HOW TO READ RESEARCH
AND
UNDERSTAND
IT

HOW TO READ RESEARCH AND UNDERSTAND IT

Paul D. Leedy
The American University
Washington, D. C.

Macmillan Publishing Co., Inc.
New York
Collier Macmillan Publishers
London

Macmillan Publishing Co., Inc.
866 Third Avenue, New York, New York 10022

Collier Macmillan Canada, Ltd.

Library of Congress Cataloging in Publication Data

Leedy, Paul D
    How to read research and understand it.

    Includes index.
    1. Research—Methodology. I. Title.
Q180.55.M4L42   001.4'2   80-13845
ISBN 0-02-369250-2

Printing: 1 2 3 4 5 6 7 8   Year: 1 2 3 4 5 6 7 8

With boundless appreciation

to

The Cheering Squad

Renie

and

The Team:

Kathy
and
Tom

A Word About This Book

Of texts dealing with research methodology, there are aplenty. But the orientation of most of these texts is toward the *production* of research. They have been written for those who, it is tacitly assumed, will ultimately write a thesis or a dissertation, and to this end such texts are slanted.

But not all courses in research are so oriented. Some are structured on the assumption that productivity of research is not necessary for all students. Some need merely an *introduction* to the research process and an *understanding* of it so that they may *read* a research report intelligently. We need not make artists of all who study art appreciation!

This book, therefore, presents research from the consumer's needs and requirements. It aims to give some appreciation for research as a methodical quest in the search for truth and the solution of problems. It aims to put into the hands of the student a research report and to point out its structure and the skills necessary to read it with insight and understanding. A chapter is devoted to the reading of graphs, charts, tables, and other non-verbal presentations that are frequently found as a part of research reporting. Few books detail the basics necessary to read with competence non-verbal graphic material of this type. The title of the book is its best description of its contents and aim.

In style and language, this book is informal. It aims to talk with the student about research—a process with which precious few students, unfortunately, are familiar. In the experience of many students, much talking has been done *about* research. Little help has been directed toward teaching them what research is and how to read it with understanding. Most of the time, they have been merely told to "go to the library to read research"—cold comfort for those who do not know how to do what they are told.

Nor is the book all talk. Periodically, as students make their way through it, they are directed to an interlude section entitled "Practical Application of the Previous Discussion." At that point, the student is given specific projects to apply in practice what has been read in theory.

This is not a big book, for the student does not need to know all of the details of selecting a sample, handling of the data, or of statistical manipulation of the data. The student does need to know, however, whether the report that is being read merits confidence and respect because it exhibits the hallmarks of research carefully designed and competently executed in practice. We should know what to look for in any report that will reveal such excellence.

The author's companion text, *Practical Research: Planning and Design*, second edition, is for those who would execute research and write reports, and for those who must fulfill requirements for graduate degrees in the writing of theses and dissertations. But that is not the mission of this volume.

The author is indebted to all of those who have suggested the need for such a text. Especially is acknowledgment due to all those who have guided this effort with their constructive criticism and their helpful suggestions. To his wife, who has been his impeccable proofreader and wise counselor, the author is indebted for a gift of patience and interest that has seen this manuscript through its long journey to its present form.

P. D. L.

Contents

CHAPTER **1**   About Research:

Those Who Produce It
Those Who Consume It

In today's world, research is inevitable. It is inevitable because problems are inevitable, and research is the process we employ to resolve problems. It is a broad avanue that leads hopefully to the discovery of truth; a means of verifying fact and of predicting outcomes. Research is an accepted mode of investigation, a way of life. The problems that beleaguer us, the situations that perplex, and the probing of the darkness of the unknown—where our knowledge fails—these situations we attempt to resolve through the medium of research. The more we advance, the more we must know, and the greater is the role that research must play.

What we call the "information explosion" is essentially the result of new knowledge discovered through the process of research. To know how to read and to understand research is, therefore, one of the basic competencies which every man and woman in the modern world should possess. It is as essential as the three R's; as important as the ability to drive a car or to use a typewriter.

And the need to develop a competency in reading and understanding research carries with it also a corollary need: that of developing a critical faculty and evaluative skills so that we may judge with fairness the *quality* of the research we are asked to accept.

A constant stream of claims in the name of research bombard us daily. Journals, newspapers, magazines, television commercials, roadway signboards are replete with phrases such as "research has found that...," "research has just discovered...," "research says...." We are advised that "research proves" that Chase-a-Cold is a product that has been "hospital-tested and found by doctors to be three times more effective in combating the symptoms of the common cold than any other product available without a prescription." Such claims confuse and mislead. They warp the meaning of the term *research* to the point where many of us are bewildered as to precisely what research is or what it is supposed to accomplish.

Such loose usage of the term *research* deprives us of standards against which to judge the quality of any research or the validity of its claims. As a result, we accept gullibly what we should have weighed critically, and we have believed where we should have questioned searchingly.

A rather crass comparison may not be out of order so that we may set our sights straight. Research is a process, and the reports of its activity are its most important product. The reports of research are the items that the research production line offers the public for acceptance or rejection. And they should be regarded as such. In consequence, we should evaluate the reporting of research as critically and inspect it as thoroughly as we would any other item of the marketplace. Shoddy research and shoddy merchandise both belong to the same unenviable category and are unworthy of serious attention. Yet, because research is so little understood, we tend to invest it willy-nilly with an aura of respect whether it merits such recognition or not.

There is no justification for regarding research as sacrosanct; nor should we be awed or intimidated by it, simply because we do not understand the research process or are unable to evaluate its merits. In a very real sense, research is a product and, like any other product, it may be of excellent quality, or it may exhibit deficiencies and defects. The quality control may not have been the best.

The purpose of this book will be, therefore, to give you some guidelines against which to judge the quality of the product which researchers offer for your attention. It will help you to ask intelligent questions about research production, to inspect knowingly its design and procedures, and to test the validity of its conclusions so that, thereby, you may be better able to judge the value of the research and appraise its worth intelligently.

RESEARCH DEALS WITH PROBLEMS

Research deals with problems, and problems are not hard to find. Medicine faces diseases whose causes are baffling and whose cures lie beyond the present knowledge and skill of medical science. Industry discovers problems distinctive to the production and performance of its products. If an industry is to stay in business, it must find a way to solve those problems, whether they concern the development of a more energy-efficient automobile or the building of a better microwave oven. And to accomplish these objectives, medicine turns to its research laboratories and industry to its research and development units. Both rely upon research to help them solve their problems.

Teachers in a classroom seek for a better and more effective way to teach boys and girls; and in seeking to resolve the problems of the classroom, they seek the findings of the latest educational research. Historians are troubled by variant readings of a manuscript or the accuracy of the writings of a history scholar. They, likewise, resort to the assistance of historical research. Wherever problems lurk, there research has an opportunity to assist in resolving the problematic situation.

From the preceding discussion, we may conclude that *the prime function of research is to deal with problems.* In fact, research *begins* with a problem. *Where there is no problem, there is no research.* And, by problems, we mean those tantalizing, enigmatical, unresolved roadblocks to knowledge and human progress for which no answer has yet been found.

ALL THAT IS CALLED RESEARCH, IS NOT RESEARCH

This is an important definition. We state it here because of the looseness with which the word *research* is used in popular communication.

Take two examples to illustrate the point. A student is sent to the library to find the composition of human blood. His instructor tells him that he expects the student to do considerable "research" in fulfilling the assignment. What the student will be doing is merely *seeking information*. He will be fact-gathering—dispelling his own ignorance of the subject; but he will not be doing research. The student has a problem indeed, but it is not a *research* problem. It is a *personal* problem: he was uninformed. His problem was not such that, because of it, he *encountered an unresolved roadblock for which there existed no answer had been found*. There was an answer to his problem, and it lay in one of the books on one of the shelves of the library. The word "research" was used by his instructor to denote nothing more than an information-seeking safari.

Take a second example. You move into a new community, and one of your first acts is to call a realtor to locate a house for you and your family. He discusses your needs and concludes by assuring you that he will "research your problem" to see if, through his "research," he can find you a suitable property. What he will actually do, in all probability, is to go to his listing of properties to see if any of the homes listed by his firm meets your requirements. He may call other realtors to inquire as to their listings. But one fact is clear: in all this activity no "research" is taking place. He is not faced with a *roadblock to knowledge and human progress for which there exists no answer whatsoever*. The realtor did not have *that* kind of problem. The realtor's problem had an answer: either he had listed the type of home that you specified—or could locate one—or he could not. It was as simple as that. But his problem posed no "roadblock to human knowledge and progress." His problem and the student's problem were merely personal problems arising out of a lack of information. Neither was concerned with research. Each was simply seeking a particular item of information which existed but which neither individually had at his immediate command.

If we are to read and understand research, we should know enough about the nature of genuine research to be able to judge the difference between what is *called* research and what really *is* research. After firmly making that distinction, we should then be able to read a research report with such critical skill as to evaluate it intelligently, and to determine how trustworthy the reported research may be, how sound its execution had been, and what credence to give to its conclusions and findings.

It is important to have such ability. Students are sent by their professors to the library to "read research." Many go without adequate guidelines to assist them in judging whether what they read is genuine research or whether it is of such poor quality in conception, in methodology, and in execution as to be scarcely worthy of the time they spend on it. For not everything that masquerades *as* research indeed *is* research—not even sometimes when it appears in respected and scholarly journals. The fact that a report is in print does not guarantee that the research underlying it has been either well done or carefully designed.

But, in any event, we must be in a position to evaluate research quality and to make a decision upon its worth. To that end, this text will aim to give you some guidelines and criteria.

--- ---

Practical Application of the Preceding Discussion

> *Reading a textbook is like listening to a sermon. Neither may be an arduous task in itself, but then neither, of itself, may reward you without further effort.*

Both should generate activities which extend beyond the mere discussion. For that reason, as you proceed through this text, you will be detoured occasionally from merely reading the text to an application of what has been discussed. For example, here are three projects which are closely related to certain items in the discussion that you have just read. They will provide an opportunity to apply what you have presumably learned.

Project 1. We have discussed the emphasis upon research as being omnipresent: in advertising, in the media, and in the world around us. (See page 1, the paragraph beginning, "A constant stream of claims. . . .") Make a collection of advertisements, articles, news stories, and television commercials which purport to report research. You will use this material in later applications. Put it in a file folder to keep it against future use. Your instructor may also ask you to discuss these in class in relation to the discussion in the text.

Project 2. We have said, "Research deals with problems, and problems are not hard to find." (page 2). Make a list of problems which you observe as needing to be solved, questions that should have answers which research investigations may provide. Write each problem on a 4-inch by 6-inch filing card. Leave ample space to add further explanation, comment, or notation. File the assignment. In a future chapter, we shall want you to do something more with each of these problems.

Project 3. Research is an attempt to remove a roadblock to knowledge and human progress. List some of the areas where roadblocks still exist. For example, a roadblock in the way of medical knowledge is a cure for muscular dystrophy. List others. Keep this list; you may need it later.

RESEARCH PRODUCERS AND RESEARCH CONSUMERS

Those concerned with research belong to one of two principal groups: either those who *produce* research, or those who *consume* research. Those of the latter group appreciate and profit from the findings of research producers. Consumers read research for various reasons: to keep abreast of latest developments in a given area, to round out their knowledge of a particular subject, or to apply what the researcher has discovered to the solution of other problems similar to those upon which the researcher has worked.

But to read research critically, you need some familiarity with the research process. Begin reading research, and you soon come upon language that you do not understand, terminology that needs translation, concepts that are unfamiliar, and statistics that are meaningless. Reference to the *t* test, to the analysis of variance, the null hypothesis, or to nonparametric statistical tests may leave the reader who is unprepared for such terminology bewildered and lost. There is more to reading and understanding a research report than merely recognizing the words upon the page.

So that you may read research intelligently, therefore, you should know something about the research process. You should know how researchers work, and you should be able

4

to comprehend the overall design and plan of attack upon the problem.[1] You should also be aware of those distinctive features that characterize quality and, conversely, what faults in planning and design result in an inferior research effort. What is the basis on which to judge soundness of research design? All these matters are important in reading and understanding research. Not everyone who can read, can read research.

There is, then, a *way* to read research. Certain information is indispensable. Both producer and consumer need to have a common body of knowledge, although each will utilize it differently. Consider, for example, the difference that exists between a text designed for those whose purpose it is to *create* art and one written expressly for those who merely seek to *appreciate* it. The users of each text need certain basic information. The artist and the devotee of art, alike, need to have a common understanding of perspective, form, texture, light and shade, and similar topics, but the text which aims to teach the student how to create a picture will present these topics in one way, and the text which intends to teach the student how to appreciate the work of art will present the same topics in quite a different way.

Just so in reading research. You may find in this text common knowledge and familiar concepts which overlap with those which are conventionally presented in so-called texts in research methodology. If so, the purpose will be merely to give you an understanding of those basic concepts and that important factual knowledge without which you cannot possibly read research intelligently.

But, to begin with, you need to see the research landscape in broad perspective. You need to appreciate those basic approaches to the acquisition of truth under the aegis of the scientific method. Before entering upon such a new area, however, let us make a practical application of some of the matters that we have been considering in the past few pages.

Practical Application of the Preceding Discussion

Project 1. Earlier in these pages (page 4) you came upon this sentence: "Begin reading research, and you soon come upon language that you do not understand, terminology that needs translation, concepts that are unfamiliar, and statistics that are meaningless." Let's see how accurate that description is in your case. Do this: (1) Go to the professional research journal serving your academic field, or relating to the academic discipline in which this text is used, and read several of the research reports. (2) Make a list of what you do not understand. (3) Organize your items under the four headings suggested in the quotation: (a) language that is baffling, (b) terminology that you do not understand, (c) concepts that are unfamiliar, and (d) statistics or statistical concepts that are meaningless to you.

---

[1]The author's companion text, *Practical Research: Planning and Design*, Second edition, (New York: Macmillan Publishing Company, Inc., 1980) is written especially for those who wish to *produce* research. The text that you are now reading is designed for those who wish to *consume*—to read and understand—research.

CHAPTER 2 Research: A Modern Way to Seek the Truth

How the Ancients Sought It
How the Middle Ages Sought It
How We Seek It Now

WHAT IS RESEARCH?

Research is an intellectual approach to an unsolved problem, and its function is to seek the truth. It is a process by which we seek to come as close as possible to elemental causes and fundamental facts. Through research, we attempt to answer the questions for which no answers exist, to solve the problems that have not as yet been solved, or to reaffirm those answers and solutions which we assume to be valid but need confirmation to make them so.

Research is essentially an attitude of mind—a way of thinking. It is the mental approach that we bring to the quest for the answer to a problem that differentiates research from other forms of truth-seeking attitudes.

Not always in the history of mankind has problem-solving been by the methodology of research. The human race has, in fact, followed several different pathways in the search for knowledge and truth.

THE SEARCH FOR KNOWLEDGE

Through myth. For the next few pages, we are going to see how man has sought for knowledge in connection with one natural phenomenon: the thunderstorm.

In the infancy of the human race, man observed the storm, was awed by it, feared its destructive force, and was curious about its origin and its meaning. He attempted to explain it—that is, to find out the truth about it through his own resources and imagination.

He invented myths, and myths grew into beliefs, and beliefs grew to become accepted answers for what otherwise would have remained a mystery.

And so, when the winds blew, and the rains came, and lightning flashed, and thunder reverberated through the sky, the "explanation" for it was that the gods were on a rampage. The winds blew because Zeus ordered Aeolus, god of the winds, to open up his "cave of the winds," letting some of them rush out to harass mankind. The lightning crackled in the sky because the gods were angry and Zeus hurled thunderbolts at them in his rage. Man had found an "answer" to explain what was unexplained and to resolve a phenomenon which he did not understand. Oversimplification and naivete? Of course! But it was an attempt at finding a solution to a problem for which they had no solution whatsoever.

But explanation by myth soon became too transparent to last. Men were becoming more sophisticated. They no longer believed in the gods.

Through reasoning. And so, following explanation by myth came explanation by *reason*. Search for truth by reason resulted from the combined influence of Greek and Christian thought. Its attitude was: Reason out the problem; find the way out of a dilemma by thinking clearly and logically. Resolve the problem in the head. And, in pursuit of truth through this means, rationalization reached its summit in syllogistic reasoning. The syllogism coexisted with the gods but supplanted them in the middle ages.

Syllogisms are, of course, merely systematic forms of reasoning. They consist of three propositions, two of which seem to be self-evident truths, generally accepted, and so obvious that no rational person would question them: God is good, man is mortal, happiness is better than sorrow. These are statements which, because of their axiomatic nature, are beyond the need for justification, substantiation, or proof. A statement in a syllogism which is its basic proposition, and axiomatic, is known as the *major premise*. A second statement which is in part an application of the major premise to a specific situation—about which also there is little room for argument—is called the *minor premise*. Issuing from these two statements, the *conclusion* is an inevitable consequence.

How, then, did the middle ages resolve the problem which had mystified the ancients. The problem was the same. Lightning flashed in the medieval sky, over monastery and castle, as it had over the Acropolis and the Roman Colosseum. How, then, would medieval man settle the matter of lightning? He saw its destructive force as had the cave man; it killed him as instantaneously as it had the ancient Greek. What answer would medieval man find to "explain" it? He would find the answer in the power of reason. The syllogism would explain the unexplainable. And it would go something like this:

> The Devil is the author of destruction and deserves to be feared.
> Lightning is a destructive and fearful force.
> Therefore, lightning is the work of the Devil.

When the gods disappeared, they were replaced in the medieval world by invisible spirits: the powers of darkness and the angels of light, and *they* were quite as real to the medieval mind as the gods had been to the ancient Greek.

Both of these approaches to the solution of problems had, however, one inherent weakness. Both originated *within* the thinking of the individual. They attempted to solve *external* problems by means of an *internal* methodology. Despite that, the ancient myth and the classical syllogism served the ancient and medieval scholars to arrive, as far as they were concerned, at a satisfactory resolution for their problem solutions.

8

What the individual thought—particularly if this coincided with a general opinion held by the people at large (e.g. God is good; man is mortal, the Devil is the cause of all evil) became the departure point for syllogistic problem solving. Its methodology was the infallibility of logic. It accomplished its purpose: it was a way to solve problems and to provide answers to unanswerable questions. It was clean, efficient, and final; and a way to seek the truth that was perfectly acceptable to the medieval mind. But its weakness was that it was *subjective* and *whimsical*.

Through the scientific method. But by the time deductive logic had reached its zenith, in the 13th century, and St. Thomas Aquinas was resolving most of the problems of earth and heaven in the *Summa Theologica*, another throughway to the discovery of truth, which was to span the centuries from the 13th to the 20th, was being opened up. This was the avenue of inductive reasoning whose methodology has come to be known as *the scientific method.*

In the 13th century, the lives of two men ran side by side. One was Thomas Aquinas, the Angelic Doctor (1225?-1274?) and high priest of rationalism. The other was Roger Bacon, the Admirable Doctor (1214?-1294) and exponent of the new learning. Here was rationalism at its classic best in stark contrast to the empirical beginnings of a new way of seeking the truth. Aquinas was the last of the great medieval scholastics who considered all discovery of truth to originate in one of two ways: dialecticism or revelation, and the *Summa* is a magnificent monument to this viewpoint.

Roger Bacon, on the other hand, stood out from his age in bold relief and his shadow fell on centuries far in advance of his time. He was a friar, a university professor, an experimentalist, and—of particular interest to us—an early advocate of the scientific method of research. These two men—contemporaries in the medieval world, yet worlds apart in their approach to the methodological solution of problems—symbolize the transition from the old thinking to the new. Feeling that he could learn more from the man in the street than from scholars in cloistered halls, Bacon championed experimentalism and predicted the invention of the airplane, the automobile, and the submarine. Further, he urged the study of mathematics to give a quantitative basis to science.[1]

He was, in fact, one of the first "Renaissance men." During the 12th and 13th centuries, the Renaissance was emerging. It grew rapidly. Basically a spirit, an attitude, an approach to life, a new way of thinking, the seeds of the Renaissance were being transported from lands far to the East—from the great universities and centers of Islamic thought: Baghdad, Bokhara, and Cairo; by Jewish and Islamic scholars: Avicenna (980-1037?), Averroës (1126-1198), Maimonides (1135-1204). The route was by the way of Spain and southern France. A clean break with the past was imminent. Its essential characteristic was the way man looked at life. Renaissance man looked, not *inside* to his own *thoughts*, but *outside*, to the *facts* of the world around him. Humanism, which was but one phase of the Renaissance, rejoiced in man—not as a child of God whose whole duty was to love Him and glorify Him forever, not as a temple of the Holy Spirit whose end was to contemplate and await revelation—but as a social individual and a biological fact. Man was an organization of bones and tissues, of specialized organs functioning in harmony with Nature's laws and in precise and predictable ways. Man was of the earth, earthy.

---

[1]Frederick Meyer, *A History of Educational Thought*, second edition. (Columbus, Ohio: Charles E. Merrill Books, Inc., 1966), pp. 500-501.

These views and this manner of thinking shook the medieval bastion of didacticism to its foundations. Much of the past had to go when the men of the Renaissance came in search of truth. The seven heavens of the ancients, stacked layer cake fashion, were outmoded and proved factually untenable. The earth-centered universe of Ptolemy and the cosmological dogmas of the medieval Church were belied by the observations of Copernicus and Galileo. Galileo peered through his telescope and *saw* the moons of Jupiter. He looked at the moon, and it was a land of plains and mountains and craters, large and small. No longer did it belong to Diana or Artemis. Copernicus shifted the center of the solar system from the earth, which was the "footstool of the Lord," to the sun because he *observed* the progress of the planets and the motions of the other heavenly bodies, and with the aid of mathematics he shattered the belief of 2000 years. Michaelangelo, inspired by the work of Vesalius and Galen, gave us a series of artistic sketches of the human body which, even by the standards of today, are reasonably accurate and anatomically correct. He drew precisely what his eyes *saw*.

Thus, the foundation for modern research was being laid. The method was simple and direct, and, ideally, uninfluenced by personal thoughts or religious beliefs. One methodology governed the new learning: Look, see, record; look again, see a second time, record once more. Believe what your eyes tell you, what your senses proclaim. That was the method. It was a method in headlong pursuit of truth by an insatiable thirst for facts. One authority was to be obeyed: the authority of the *observing eye*, the *listening ear*, the *impression of the senses*. A search for truth through the accurate observation and interpretation of fact is what we have come to know as *the scientific method*. It is the method of modern research. Observation and experimentation, and confirmation of one's findings by replication, supplanted the pursuit of truth by pure reason.

We have seen how mythology and medieval dialectic would have resolved the common phenomenon of the thunderstorm. Now, we shall see how those dedicated to the tenets of the scientific method also dealt with the same event. The phenomenon had lost none of its appeal.

Lightning fascinated the men of the 18th century quite as tantalizingly as it had intrigued the mind of early man or that of the middle ages. But to the 18th-century mind, the earlier explanations of lightning were too simplistic and naive. Eighteenth-century man had a different approach to the problem entirely. He studied nature and observed the way nature behaved. He gathered facts from the world around him and used such facts as a means of resolving the problems that confronted him. Through *observation* and *collection of factual data*, guided by a reasonable *hypothesis*, he would discover the truth about lightning: its character, its cause, its explanation.

Its destructiveness commanded attention as a force that needed to be understood and, if possible, controlled. Benjamin Franklin addressed himself to the problem. He had a "hunch" (a hypothesis) that lightning was "electrical fire"—electricity being as much in the forefront of the popular mind of those days as atomic energy is in our day.

To test his hypothesis, Franklin took the first opportunity to get the *facts*. Noticing an approaching thunderstorm in June 1752, he headed for an open field—string and kite in hand. In the field was a shed. With the help of his son, Franklin raised his kite into the jaws of the storm and took shelter in the shed. The string attached to the kite, he tied to the doorknob. After some time, he noticed the loose threads of the hempen string standing erect. Struck with this promising sign, he immediately presented his knuckle to the key in the door. The discovery was quick and conclusive. The sting of an electric spark, blue and crackling, snapped at his knuckle. The facts were indisputable—it *was* "electric fire"!

Franklin had established that what came from the clouds appeared to be identical with what he observed when glass was rubbed with silk or resin with wool or fur. With these materials he could also produce a spark—feeble in comparison, but identical in nature, with that which he drew from the clouds.[2]

THE RESEARCH PROCESS

This classic experiment is a perfect example of the scientific method at work and of a primitive research design. It is a summary of all that comprises a research project. We might skeletonize it by the following chainlike series of events. For this, in abbreviated form *is* research:

Curiosity

↓

A hunch (hypothesis)

↓

Getting the facts to test the hypothesis

↓

The facts confirm (or do not confirm) the hypothesis

↓

The facts lead to a conclusion which satisfies your original curiosity.

Briefly, that is the scientific method; that is research.

Our review of the quest for knowledge has ended in a search for *facts*. For, facts alone must solve problems, answer questions, and let us see clearly what the conditions in the world around us really are. But the "world" of facts and the geographical globe are two entirely different things. When we speak of "the world of facts" which are relevant to the unsolved problem, we mean a context in which the facts exist. This world may be a natural, social, physical, historical, biological, economic, environmental world or one of any other character. Such a "world" out of which facts arise is commonly called in research a *universe* or *population*. And you will probably meet these terms many times in reading research reports.

Also, we should clarify another misconception with respect to the facts. We emphasize many times the importance of the collection or the acquisition of the *data* (which is a word used in research for *facts*). But we overlook the fact that this is merely *half* of the research process. Research is not gathering together an accumulation of facts for the purpose of having an accumulation of facts. The much more important half is the *study of the accumulated data*, which is known to researchers as the *interpretation of the data*. Interpretation is the key to the whole research effort. We shall look at it carefully in succeeding pages of this book.

But, for the moment, and because the scientific method is so very important as the foundation of all modern research activity, we present it here in outline form, indicating its principal characteristics and illustrating these from the discussion that you have just read.

---

[2]See Joseph Priestley, *History and Present State of Electricity*, second edition. (London, 1769), pp. 171–172. See also Carl van Doren, *Benjamin Franklin*. (New York: The Viking Press, 1938), pp. 164–167.

SUMMARY OF THE CHARACTERISTICS OF
THE SCIENTIFIC METHOD

Steps in the Scientific Method	*Comments and Examples*
1. The scientific method begins with curiosity about a given situation which is articulated as a *problem* frequently phrased in the form of a *question*.	Lightning: What is it? What causes it? What are its characteristics or its nature?
2. The investigator (or researcher) formulates a *hypothesis*; that is, an educated guess, a "hunch."	The hypothesis directs the thinking of the researcher. Franklin guessed that lightning was "electrical fire."
3. The scientific method gathers information (facts, or data) *by observation* relevant to the phenomenon under investigation.	Franklin flew his kite in the face of the storm to gather information about the lightning.
4. The scientific method then organizes and quantifies the data so that they be easily analyzed and *interpreted*.	In the Franklin experiment, there was very little organization of the data. However, Franklin did make a sensory comparison between the "electrical fire" generated by the lightning and that generated by silk rubbed on glass.
5. The scientific method draws conclusions on the basis of observed fact only. The factual chips must fall where they may!	Because of the similarity and sensations between one spark and the other, Franklin concluded that lightning was, indeed, "electrical fire." Hypothesis was sustained.
6. The process of investigation can be repeated (replicated) with high expectation that, if all factors are identical, and all conditions are strictly observed, the results will be comparable to those secured at the first investigation of the problem.	Those without fear may also go out in open fields and fly kites into thunderstorms and, by attaching "a hempen string" to a shed doorknob may still expect to draw sparks from key to knuckle—and, in all probability, will!

And so, to this point, we have been considering in chapters 1 and 2 the broad base for understanding research generally. Now, we shall look at specific aspects of reading and understanding research as we meet it in journal literature, reports, and other published sources of research output. But first, let's apply the material presented in the foregoing discussion.

— —

Practical Application of the Preceding Discussion

Project 1. We have discussed how one natural phenomenon (lightning) was "explained" by the ancients in terms of mythology. Mythology resolved many problems in much the same way. Make a list of all the phenomena that you can recall which were "explained" through the actions of mythological characters. You may wish to consult Bullfinch, Mythology or encyclopedia articles under the heading of "Mythology" to assist you in this assignment.

Project 2. Take one or more of the phenomena which you have listed above and show how we have gained insight into the real nature of the phenomenon through the application of the scientific method. You may wish to combine both of these projects into one presentation by using a form similar to the one suggested here.

Phenomenon	Mythological Explanation	Scientific Explanation
Example: Lightning	The anger of the gods.	Accumulation of static electricity of opposite polarities and discharging by means of an electric "spark."

CHAPTER 3

Research Reports:

What Are They?
Where Do You Find Them?
How Do You Read Them?

For most of us, research is an elusive matter. To the average person, the word research has about it an aura of mystery, an esoteric glow. We hear the word repeatedly on TV, in the news columns, in advertising; but most of us know very little about the nature of research, or what researchers actually do. For most of us, researchers are elusive beings with whom we have had little or no personal contact. Perhaps, if someone asked you to write down the name of a researcher at this moment with whom you have had personal contact, you would be at a loss to name one. With other professions the situation is different. We would have no such difficulty with identifying a physician, an attorney, a clergyman, a teacher. With these people and their work we have intimate knowledge. Researchers? We are at a dead-end street.

Yet every year, billions of dollars are spent on what researchers do, and thousands of men and women arise each morning to go off to a day's activity in the area of one form of research or another. This results in a deluge of research reporting. Every day sees literally tons of reports issued from the printing presses of the world. Elusive though it may seem, the research process is very real. Even while you read these words, discoveries are being made, and new knowledge is being generated at an explosive rate. We are in an expanding universe of factual discovery, and the evidence of it is the deluge of *research reports* that are issued to inform us concerning it.

THE RESEARCH REPORT

But what is a research report? *A research report is a document that sets forth clearly and specifically what the researcher has done, including a statement of the situation which initiated the research, precisely what problem the researcher was attempting to resolve, how the data were controlled and gathered, how the data have been organized and studied for analysis and interpretation, and what results have been obtained including the conclusions that the study of the data has dictated.* Research reports are, therefore, a clear exposition of what researchers do and how they do it. Most reports follow a somewhat standard format, and they usually include a standard agenda of topics. Some variation in presentation is common, but certain items within the report are necessary so that we may get a clear perspective as to what the researcher has done and how he has done it.

So that you may know what to look for when you read a research report, we shall list and discuss briefly the usual topics covered.

The Parts of a Research Report

1. *The title and other heading material.* The report usually begins with a title, stating the subject with which the report will deal. The name of the researcher and professional affiliation is also a part of the title material.

2. *An abstract of the reported research.* Many research reports begin with an abstract, some do not. The abstract gives a summary or overview of the entire research endeavor. This part of the report assists the reader to get a miniature reporting of the entire project, thus helping the reader to decide whether he wishes to read further.

3. *The introduction.* The introduction to the report proper usually consists of a paragraph, or several paragraphs, which aim to give some justification for the research being reported. It may include a review of antecedent research by others, a *raison d'être* for the research which is being reported, an indication of its importance or relevance to existing practical problems, and its relation to other existing research.

4. *The statement of the research goal.* Every report should set forth clearly, either by obvious implication or by direct statement, the problem which forms the heart of the research effort. What was the researcher attempting to do? What is the problem for which he was seeking a solution? What undiscovered knowledge was he trying to find? What was the purpose of the research project? The report should set forth the problem clearly so that we have no doubt as to what the researcher was attempting to do.

   On page 17 is a part of a research report from *Dissertation Abstracts International.*[1] Notice how the author immediately sets before the reader the purpose—the problem—of the research endeavor.

   Carefully written research reports always inform the reader precisely what the problem was that has been researched. *This is one of the first items to look for when reading any reporting of research.* Failure to delineate the problem clearly for the reader reflects upon the quality of the report, but more seriously it hints at the ability of the researcher writing the report to think without confusion clearly—to put first things first. Language is the mirror of the mind. Reports that ramble, that fail to zoom in, isolating the central research objective, setting it forth appropriately and adequately in unmistakable terms, unfortunately raise a presumption that the quality of the research itself may

---

[1]*Op. cit.,* Vol. 39 (July, 1978), p. 366-B. Dissertation in General Psychology.

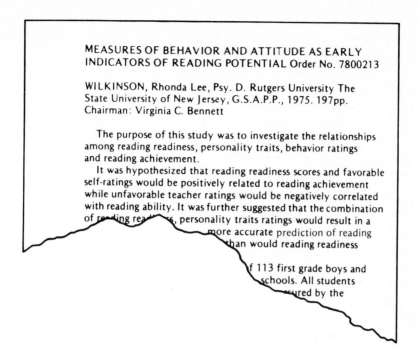

MEASURES OF BEHAVIOR AND ATTITUDE AS EARLY
INDICATORS OF READING POTENTIAL Order No. 7800213

WILKINSON, Rhonda Lee, Psy. D. Rutgers University The
State University of New Jersey, G.S.A.P.P., 1975. 197pp.
Chairman: Virginia C. Bennett

The purpose of this study was to investigate the relationships
among reading readiness, personality traits, behavior ratings
and reading achievement.
It was hypothesized that reading readiness scores and favorable
self-ratings would be positively related to reading achievement
while unfavorable teacher ratings would be negatively correlated
with reading ability. It was further suggested that the combination
of reading readiness, personality traits ratings would result in a
more accurate prediction of reading
than would reading readiness

f 113 first grade boys and
schools. All students
red by the

have a possible kinship with the verbal fog found in the report. Reportorial
haze should alert you to read the rest of the report with circumspection and
with more than usual care.

5. *Related research.* Throughout the report, and especially in the introductory
section, the efforts of others are acknowledged and their relevancy to the research being reported is indicated. Those who engage in research are quite
cognizant that the work of others assists them in resolving their own problems. No research effort is ever an isolated quest.

The manner in which reference to related research is indicated varies, but,
in general, there are two major types of reference. Sometimes reference to the
work of others is noted by employing a number—usually in parentheses—following the citation. This number refers to the comparably numbered item in
the list of references at the end of the report. An example of this type of documentation is seen in the following illustration which is the introduction to a
report in *Science.*[2] The research was an investigation into the phenomenon of
lake monsters, of which the Loch Ness monster is perhaps the most famous.
The problem was: How can we account for the seemingly very real appearance
of these monsters? On the next page is the opening of the report, and the list
of references and notes which was appended to the end of the article.

Related research literature references may also use a different style: the
name or names of the researchers, followed by the year of publication of their
research report. The excerpt on page 19, from a report in the *Journal of
Counseling Psychology*, will illustrate this form of citation.[3]

---

[2]*Science,* Vol. 205 (July 13, 1979), pp. 183–185.

[3]Don Knowles, "On the Tendency for Volunteer Helpers to Give Advice," *Journal of Counseling Psychology*, 1979, Vol. 26, No. 4, pp. 352–354.

Atmospheric Refraction and Lake Monsters

Abstract. *A survey of reported sightings of lake monster phenomena suggests that many of them may be attributable to atmospheric image distortion. The existence of the necessary conditions (surface temperature inversion and hence strong atmospheric refraction) can be inferred from most of the reports. Under such conditions familiar objects can easily take on unrecognizable form. Two photographs demonstrate the extent of the distortion that can occur.*

Lake monsters have been a part of legend among many peoples. Modern sightings, too frequent to be ignored, have intrigued many scientists, with the result that the subject of lake (and sea) monsters has become the focus of some serious research. Gould (*1*), Mackal (*2*), and others have collected enough careful reports from reputable eyewitnesses to dispel any doubt that the observers were indeed seeing unusual phenomena.

The one element missing from all of these reports (with the exception of Mackal's brief and somewhat incomplete appendix on mirages) is any consideration that the observed or photographed evidence might have been optically distorted by the atmosphere. It may well be that many sightings of monsters can be explained as the sighting of a distorted and hence unrecognized image of a familiar creature or phenomenon.

In the same way that Mackal carefully weeds out much "evidence" as representing standing waves, birds, otters, and so on, it may be possible to accomplish some further weeding-out on the basis of image distortion.

It is well known that approximately horizontal light rays are refracted slightly downward, toward the denser layers of the atmosphere (*3*). This refraction can become strong enough to cause visible distortions if a temperature inversion is present to steepen the density gradient near the earth's surface (*4*). Very interesting cases arise when the ⸻gradient is nonuniform with ⸻ point on the object ⸻ for several rays, ⸻'s eye at dif- ⸻assumes ⸻ight; ⸻ a

References and Notes

1. R. T. Gould, *The Case for the Sea Serpent* (Philip Allan, London, 1930).
2. R. P. Mackal, *The Monsters of Loch Ness* (Swallow, Chicago, 1976).
3. An extensive literature exists. On atmospheric refraction, see texts such as J. M. Pernter and F. M. Exner, *Meteorologische Optik* (Braumüller, Vienna, 1922); M. Minnaert, *Light and Colour in the Open Air* (Bell, London, 1940); W. J. Humphreys, *Physics of the Air* (Dover, New York, 1964); H. R. Reed and C. M. Russell, *Ultra High Frequency Propagation* (Boston Technical Publishers, Cambridge, 1966). On image distortion see, for example, A. B. Fraser, *Appl. Opt.* **14**, A92 (1975); W. H. Lehn and H. L. Sawatzky, *Polarforschung* **45**, 120 (1975); W. H. Lehn and M. B. El-Arini, *Appl. Opt.* **17**, 3146 (1978); W. H. Lehn, *J. Opt. Soc. Am.*, in press.
4. The curvature of a nearly horizontal ray is approximately proportional to the temperature gradient. As an example, if the surface temperature is 0°C, an inversion with the relatively mild gradient of 0.11°C/m is sufficient to produce rays with the same curvature as the earth's.
5. See, for example, I. P. Koch, *Medd. Groenl.* **46**, 191 (1917); J. P. Koch and A. Wegener, *ibid.* **75**, 610 (1930). I have similarly made frequent observations of such zones of vertical distension. ⸻ostello, *In Search of Lake Monsters* (Garn⸻ London, 1974), p. 290. ⸻and photographed numerous ⸻anitoba and Winnipeg. One ⸻as made by chance while ⸻ a hot day (7 Au- ⸻rip appeared ⸻utes, at

Data collected over a 3-year period from volunteers to a telephone crisis-line service were considered in the present study. Of particular interest was the quality of helping-intended responses given by volunteers when they first arrived at the agency. The expectation of providing help to callers may be so pronounced that the agency's goals of wanting the caller to feel respected and understood are jeopardized.

One difficulty arises when assistance is given in a manner which implies incompetence on the part of the recipient, thereby producing feelings of being a failure and resentment toward both the help and the person who provided it (Berkowitz & Connor, 1966). Further, overly ambitious offers of assistance convey a lack of respect for the recipient's ability to meet the demands of a situation (Carkhuff, 1969). The recipient may al-

so interpret the assistance to mean that his or her own feelings and experiences are not important.

The development of *response mode categories* by Goodman and Dooley (1976) provided a framework for studying the type of communication offered in crisis-line conversations and counseling interviews. Six basic response categories have been identified: question, advisement, silence, interpretation, reflection, and self-disclosure. Of particular interest in the present study were advisements, an appropriate type of response for eliciting well-defined behavior but ineffective in eliciting rapport of encouraging self-exploration. What was being sought in responses of volunteers to the initial phase of a call was a high proportion of reflection statements and a low proportion of advisement statements.

References

Berkowitz, L., & Connor, W. H. Success, failure, and social responsibility. *Journal of Personality and Social Psychology*, 1966, *4*, 664–669.

Carkhuff, R. R. *Helping and human relations: A primer for lay and professional helpers: Vol. 1. Selection and training.* Toronto: Holt, Rinehart & Winston, 1969.

Goodman, G., & Dooley, D. A framework for help-intended communication. *Psychotherapy*, 1976, *13*, 106–117.

Whalen, C. K., & Flowers, J. V. Effects of role and gender mix on verbal communication modes. *Journal of Counseling Psychology*, 1977, *24*, 281–287.

6. *The method and design of the research.* The research *method* is the way in which the researcher gathers the data and analyzes them so that they will reveal their meaning. We shall list briefly the various methods of research with a brief explanation of each. While research methodology goes under a variety of names, basic processes by which data are processed may be described under four general headings.

   (a) *The descriptive, or normative, survey method.* Employing this method, the researcher gathers data by *observation* or by *surveying* the research universe[4]; and then, usually by means of simple statistics, seeks to discover what the data seem to indicate.

---

[4] See page 11.

(b) *The statistical-analysis method.* This method of gathering and process-ing the data employs statistics—usually inferential statistics—to force the data to reveal their meaning.

(c) *The experimental method.* In the experimental method, one group of subjects is controlled by the researcher, while another and similar group is submitted to some influence, called a *variable*. The data of the two groups are then compared to determine whether the addition of the var-iable has had any effect on the outcome. If the experimental group—the group subjected to the variable—differs from the control group—the group that had nothing done to them—then it can be presumed that the variable is responsible for the difference between the two groups.

(d) *The historical method.* In this method, the data are usually in the form of historical records or documents: letters, records of events, diaries, written memoranda, artifacts, or other documentary remains. Given these documents, the historical method seems to inspect them critically so that from these documentary data, unsolved historical or philosoph-ical problems may be resolved or new facts of historical importance discovered.

In the research report, under the heading of *method*, many researchers also report other items, two of the most common of which are a description of the *subjects* used in the research project and the method employed in their selec-tion. A discussion of the *procedure* used to collect, process, and interpret the data as well as other matters may also be introduced under the heading of "method." These may include the criteria which have been used for the ad-missibility of data into the study, the precautions which have been taken to safeguard against contamination of the data by the influence of bias, or other precautions which have been taken to insure objectivity and impartiality in the study. These are all appropriate considerations under the heading of method or under any of its subheadings. And the careful researcher will usu-ally delineate somewhere in his report his safeguarding of the integrity of the study by noting these matters.

Sometimes, under the general heading of method, researchers discuss the way in which they have gathered the data, the instruments employed, the ma-terials used, or corollary studies which have provided standards or evaluate scales for the processing of the data. Under method, in fact, any facts perti-nent to the initiation or the execution of the study may be appropriately dis-cussed.

7. *The results.* In this section, the researcher sets forth the interpretations which the data seem to warrant. If the research was guided by hypotheses, here is where a statement is made as to whether the data supported or rejected those hypotheses. In statistical studies where the null hypothesis is tested, the statis-tical value established for either accepting or rejecting the hypothesis is given and the reader is advised whether the hypothesis was confirmed or rejected.

8. *The discussion.* The discussion section of a research report frequently contains a brief recapitulation of the entire research process. Here also the problem

which formed the basis for the research endeavor is resolved. The conclusions—warranted by the data—are stated. The researcher may suggest the applicability of the research findings to specific life situations, or note other conclusions which are ancillary to the main problem but which the data may have revealed and are significant enough to merit comment.

Concluding the discussion section, suggestions for additional projects which may supplement the research being reported may also be offered.

9. *Notes and references.* The final section of any research report is a listing of the documentary sources indicated within the body of the report. We have already discussed these under item 5, "Related research."[5] Within this listing may be items that are either comments of the author or informational footnotes. They are there to amplify the discussion but have no documentary reference quality.

WHERE TO FIND RESEARCH REPORTS

This chapter considers three questions with respect to research reports: What are they? Where do you find them? How do you read them? The first of these we have already answered. Now we shall address the second. The purpose of this section will be to explore where research reports are found.

Earlier, we indicated that the presses of the world pour forth tons of reported research daily.[6] This torrent of material engulfs us in a factual knowledge avalanche. Yet, despite this, ask the average person to locate a research report and, in most instances, you will be met with an incredulous blank stare. It is an assignment that few of us have ever been asked to fulfill. Go one step further: ask the same person to find a research report dealing with a particular phase of a specific subject—the relationship, for example, of stress to the incidence of cancer—and the assignment to many will appear insurmountable.

Yet, for those who know certain throughways into the domain of learning, the task is not as impossible nor the demand as unreasonable as it at first appears.

But where does one find research reports? Where is research published? Literally, thousands of channels exist for directing the world's research to the attention of all of us. Within these pages to try to list even a small fraction of these sources would occupy the remainder of this book. But there is a way to circumvent this. Within broad limits, and by dealing with general avenues of approach, we may suggest some of the most common routes to sources that report what researchers are finding in the way of new knowledge and newly discovered truth.

Briefly, we shall suggest that you become familiar with the following channels for reporting research:

The popular reportorial media
The standard indexes
Bibliographic sources

---

[5] See pages 17–19.

[6] See page 15.

Abstracts
Reviews of research in specific fields.

The popular reportorial media. The daily newspapers, the news magazines, radio, television, and promotional advertising are perhaps the most common, and the least scientific, of all channels for reporting research. But with all their shortcomings, through these channels significant research findings sometimes do filter down to the level of popular consumption. As we indicated earlier,[7] much that is termed research bears little or no resemblance to genuine research activity, and advertisers frequently make claims in the name of research which are highly dubious.

But aside from these spurious voices, some genuine research reporting does, in fact, reach us through the popular press. The accounts are usually brief and undocumented, but they may give us a clue as to the activity which is almost certainly reported at greater length in the professional journals elsewhere. An account, occupying a few inches of newspaper column, may distill into a few words years of research activity and announce a major breakthrough in the search for answers to some unresolved and puzzling problems. News releases usually give the source of their information so that the reader, if he so wishes, may continue his quest by going to the source so quoted.

Here, for example, is a brief report dealing with research that explored the relationship of stress to the incidence of cancer. It is, in many respects, a miniature research report.

Stress and Cancer

Can emotional stress promote cancer? This question has been studied and debated for years, but there has been no consensus. Anecdotes about individuals hint strongly that there is a link, but research results have been inconsistent and often contradictory.

New experiments with mice suggest there is a link and offer a possible explanation of the previous contradictions. In the experiments, only inescapable stress enhanced cancer growth and shortened the lives of the cancer-bearing animals.

Psychologists at Carleton University in Ottawa injected mice with live cancer cells. Some of the mice were given frightening electrical shocks that they could not avoid. Other mice had a way to escape the shocks. The duration and severity of the shocks were the same. The two groups showed marked differences in development of the cancer cells. In the group that was unable to cope with stress, the animals had detectable tumors earlier, their cancers grew larger and the animals tended to die somewhat sooner than in the group that could escape, said the research team's report in a recent issue of Science, the weekly journal of the American Association for the Advancement of Science.

"The results," said the report, "strongly indicate that inability to cope with the stress behaviorally, rather than the physical stress per se, was responsible for the effects of shock on tumor size."

---

[7] See pages 2–3.

That announcement from the science section of *The New York Times*[8] contains the essential features of a formal research report. These features, which we have discussed in some detail earlier in this chapter,[9] have been italicized here for easy identification.

The *Times* release sets forth the *problem* which arose out of an issue which "has been studied and debated for years" without apparent resolution. It outlines briefly the study *population*—the *subjects* of the study (laboratory mice); it sketches briefly the *procedure* employed in the experiment (Mice were injected with cancer cells after which some were subjected to stress in the form of electrical shock from which they could not escape; others were subjected to similar stress from which they could escape, and the *results* of the experiment were set forth, with certain *conclusions* that seemed warranted by the facts as these were observed by the researchers. (The group unable to cope with stress had a greater incidence of cancer and in more aggravated form than those mice who could escape the stressful situations.)

This is perhaps the briefest and most popular form of research reporting. Note that the author of this release indicates that the source of his information is from a "report in a recent issue of *Science*, the weekly journal of the American Association for the Advancement of Science.

Indexes. Indexes are listings, without comment, of titles of published documents, together with their respective sources. An interesting project may be to go to *The New York Times Index* for any one year and look under the heading of "Research." We have done precisely this for the year 1977 and under the heading of "Science and Technology—Research"[10] area, here is what we found. Other areas: medicine, nursing, agriculture, business, and so on would probably have shown specialized research pertinent to each area.

> **SCIENCE and Technology. See also** Colls—NJ—Community Colleges, Je 2. Educ—US—Grading of Students, Je 27. Inventions. Inst, museum and school names. Names of industries and products and other specific subjects of research or application. Specific branches and disciplines
> **Research. See also** subhead China, People's Republic of, My 28. Subhead US, Je 21
> John Leonard revs Prof George A Miller book Spontaneous Apprentices: Children and Language, about experiment with 3-yr-olds in attempt to learn about growth of vocabulary (M), Ap 9,VII,p3
> Article in series describing creative process of scientific research focuses on work of Natl Institutes of Health research team headed by Dr Jesse Roth into problems of receptor disease that may be linked to diabetes and obesity; illus (L), Ap 11,24:1
> Article in series describing creative process of scientific research focuses on work of John P Snyder, NJ chem engineer with no formal training in mapping tech who has developed set of math equations by which images of Earth, taken by spacecraft, can be converted to accurate maps (L), My 20,21:1; article in series describing creative process of scientific research centers on work of Lawrence Berkeley Laboratory scientific team, headed by Dr Glenn T Seaborg, in attempting to discover super-heavy element; illus; chart (L), Je 13,II,1:1
> Article in series describing creative process of scientific research focuses on work of Johns Hopkins Univ Dr Daniel B Drachman into nature of myasthenia gravis; illus (L), Je 29,II,4:1

---

[8] *The New York Times*, August 28, 1979, section C, p. 2, column 5.
[9] See pages 16-21.
[10] *The New York Times Index, 1977*, p. 1180.

Any complete library will have a variety of indexes for various periodicals and fields of knowledge: *Index of Science and Technology, Index Medicus, Science Citation Index, Education Index, Social Science Index, Humanities Index, Public Affairs Information Service Bulletin, Business Periodicals Index, Readers' Guide to Periodical Literature*, to name just a few. Look in any of these under the heading, *Research.* You may be amazed at what you uncover. Remember also that the indexes are usually published each year and many of them appear serially each month. The annual volume that you consult is merely a compilation of the serial issues, and any one volume will contain the reported research studies for that *one year* only.

Bibliographies. Another source that students frequently overlook in locating research within a particular academic or subject area is the specialized bibliographical literature. Go to the reference section of the library and look for the *Bibliographic Index.* This is a general work and a baseline from which to begin the exploration of bibliographic literature. See if your library has the quarterly checklists of bibliography in various areas: *Quarterly Check List of Ethnology and Sociology, Quarterly Check List of Geophysics, Quarterly Check List of Linguistics, Quarterly Check List of Literary History,* and so on. If you are interested in the humanities, and especially research in English literature and language, do not overlook the *Modern Language Association: Year's Studies in English.*

Go to the card catalog. Look under *bibliography.* See what bibliographical publications your library owns. Explore them—especially those in your particular field of interest.

And, finally, do not overlook the documentary bibliographies that are listed under the heading of "References" and appended to every research report. They are a select list of bibliographical items, closely related to the area of the research being reported. Such bibliographical items are valuable in providing a global view of previous research done in the particular area of the report, and upon which the research described in the report to which they are appended may be either a replication or a further development.

Abstracts. An abstract is a summary or précis of a published document. Frequently, research reports will have an abstract immediately following the title of the report and author's name. It gives you a brief summary which is of particular value in helping you to decide whether you wish to read further into the report itself. However, abstracts are published separately and each scholarly area usually has a publication devoted to the abstracts related to that particular area. Explore such common abstracts as *Psychological Abstracts, Biological Abstracts, Child Development Abstracts and Bibliography, Education Abstracts, Chemical Abstracts,* and, of course, *Dissertation Abstracts International.*

Perhaps the best place for you to begin your study of abstracts is with *Dissertation Abstracts International.* This is a voluminous work. In it are published the abstracts of doctoral dissertations which have been accepted by graduate faculties of the major universities. Candidates for the doctorate usually write, as a partial requirement for the degree, an extended document, reporting the original research which they have done under the guidance of a faculty committee. Such dissertations comprise a sizable contribution to the research literature of every academic discipline. Most dissertations are "published" in microfilm by University Microfilms, Inc., Ann Arbor, Michigan. Concurrently with the completion of the dissertation, the student for the doctorate also prepares a summary, or abstract, of his research endeavor. These abstracts are then published in *Dissertation Abstracts International.* The work is issued in various sections, each of which is devoted to the abstracts of dissertations produced in associated disciplines of a broad academic area: the biological and physical sciences, the humanities and social sciences, and so on.

Reviews of research. The review of research is precisely what the name implies. It is an article or, in the case of journals, a publication devoted exclusively to a critical overview of the research literature in a specific area. The review of research surveys the research that has been done in a particular area and comments upon it as a body of activity indicating trends, new approaches, special emphases, or new departures in the research activity of that particular field. The reviews of research keep us informed as to the progress which is being made in a particular area of research effort, or it places current research in an historical perspective so that we may more easily appreciate the growth and sophistication of investigative studies within a specific area.

The best way to appreciate the nature of the review of research is to explore such publications directly. Consult the *Review of Educational Research*, published quarterly by the American Educational Research Association, or the *Review of the Year's Work in English Studies*, published by the Modern Language Association. They will introduce you to the review of research as a type of research bibliography, with comments and interpretations of the substantive and methodological issues and trends in research in education or English studies.

Computer search. Great quantities of information can be discovered by initiating a computer search for information. Many such search systems are now in operation. Their function is to gather and store information electronically and these data may be retrieved through normal computer search procedures. Throughout the United States, a series of centers known under their anagram designations, such as ERIC (Educational Resources Information Centers) gather, codify, and store titles, abstracts, and complete documents relating to all areas of education. Documents are issued in microfiche, and many libraries throughout the country are repositories for such microfiche collection. By instituting a search by author, title, subject, or any of the corollary designations—as indicated in the thesaurus to the system, information and documents may be located and retrieved. Printouts may be made of microfiche reproductions, so that any document may be available in printed copy.

Of similar design, and serving the medical and health sciences area, is MEDLARS (Medical Literature Analysis and Retrieval System), whose resources are devoted principally to medical, dental, nursing, and allied health science literature and research. For those who wish to make a comprehensive search for documents and reports, these two basic computer-assisted retrieval systems should not be overlooked, together with others designed for location and retrieval of specific information in areas other than education and the health sciences.

In addition to the ERIC and MEDLARS data bases, which we have just mentioned, a list of additional data-retrieval sources may be helpful.

Data Base	*Description of Material Covered*
AGRICOLA (Agricultural on-line access)	Worldwide literature in agriculture and related areas. Journals, monographs, pamphlets, reports.
AIM/ARM (Abstracts of instructional and research materials)	Literature coverage of vocational and technical education, manpower economics, employment, etc. Instructional materials.
America: History and Life	Comprehensive literature on U.S. and Canadian history and culture; current affairs and area studies. Journals, monographs, dissertations.

Data Base	*Description of Material Covered*
Art Modern	Literature of modern art and design from 1800 to the present. Journals, dissertations, exhibition catalogs, books.
CA (Chemical Abstracts)	Worldwide literature in chemistry and chemical engineering. Journals, books, reviews, patents.
Child Abuse and Neglect	English language material on the literature of child abuse and neglect. Journals, on-going research, reports, service program listings.
CRIS (Current research information system)	USDA and state-sponsored research in agriculture and related sciences. Research projects.
ENVIROLINE (Environmental sciences index)	Worldwide coverage of literature in environmental studies. Journals, news releases, reports.
ERD-RIP (Energy R&D projects)	Current U.S. energy-related research covering all energy sources. Technical reports.
FSTA (Food science and technology abstracts)	Literature of research and development in food science and technology. Journals, monographs.
GEOREF (Geological reference file)	Worldwide coverage of the literature of the geosciences. Journals, proceedings, theses.
Historical Abstracts	Worldwide coverage of the literature of history and related social sciences and humanities.
The Information Bank	News and editorial information from the *New York Times*, plus other newspapers and magazines.
Language and Language Behavior Abstracts	Worldwide literature on language and language behavior. Journals, monographs.
MEDLINE (Medlars-on-line)	Worldwide coverage of the literature of the biomedical sciences. Journals, monographs.
MRIS Abstracts (Marine Research Information Service)	Comprehensive information on maritime research and the maritime industry. Journals, on-going research, technical reports.
PAIS (Public Affairs Information Service)	Comprehensive coverage of all fields of the social sciences including political science, banking, public administration, etc.
PA (Psychological Abstracts)	Worldwide literature of psychology and the behavioral sciences. Journals, reports, monographs.
SCISEARCH (Science Citation Index)	Multidisciplinary index to the literature of science and technology. Journals, research.

Data Base	*Description of Material Covered*
SOCIAL SCISEARCH	Worldwide literature of the social sciences and humanities. Journals, research.
SSIE (Smithsonian Science Information Exchange)	Reports of government and privately funded scientific research projects. Ongoing research.
WRA (Water Resources Abstracts)	Literature on water-related aspects of the life, physical, and social sciences. Monographs, journals, reports.

The above list was excerpted from Diane Cunningham, *Data Bases Available at the National Bureau of Standards Library*, Washington, D.C. 20234, March, 1979.

For those students who are more seriously interested in locating research studies, and seeking sources which will guide them to many areas of varied information, the following guides should prove particularly useful. Anyone seriously interested in research should know these standard guides to informational sources.

Kruzas, Anthony T., editor and Linda Varenkamp Sullivan, associate editor, *Encyclopedia of Information Systems and Services*. Third Edition. Detroit, Michigan: Gale Research Co., 1978.

A guide to information storage and retrieval services, data base producers and publishers, online vendors, computer service companies, computerized retrieval systems, micrographic firms, libraries, government agencies, networks and consortia, information centers, data banks, clearinghouses, research centers, associations, and consultants.

Klein, Bernard, editor. *Guide to American Directories*. Ninth edition. Coral Springs, Florida: B. Klein Publications, Inc., 1975.

A guide to the major directories of the United States, covering all industrial, professional, and mercantile categories. Known to thousands as the "Directory of Directories."

Winchell, Constance M., *Guide to Reference Books*. Eighth edition, 1967. Chicago, Ill.: American Library Association, 1967.

A work that has had a long and distinguished history. Begun in 1902, it has become a standard reference manual in listing the reference works basic to research —general and special—listing some 7500 titles.

Information Market Place 1978-79: An International Directory of Information Products and Services. Consultant editors: European Association of Information Services and James B. Sanders. New York: R. R. Bowker Company, 1978.

Palmer, Archie M., editor and Laura E. Bryant, *Research Centers Directory*. Sixth edition. Detroit, Michigan: Gale Research Company, 1979.

A guide to university-related and other nonprofit research organizations established on a permanent basis and carrying on continuing research programs in agriculture, business, conservation, education, engineering and technology, government, law, life sciences, mathematics, area studies, physical and earth sciences, social sciences and humanities.

A collateral reference to those listed above, and of especial use to those interested in preparing research programs and encoding information is a publication by the Information Resources Press:

Lancaster, F. W., *Vocabulary Control for Information Retrieval*. Washington, D.C.: Information Resources Press, 1972.

This book deals with properties of vocabularies for indexing and searching document collections; the construction, organization, display, and maintenance of these vocabularies; and the vocabulary as a factor affecting the performance of retrieval systems.

This chapter opened with the suggestion that for most of us research and the work of the researcher were a somewhat shadowy realm into which most of us had never ventured very far. At this point you should feel more comfortable in finding your way around. You now know what research is, how researchers carry on their activity, and where the reports that represent the result of their labor may be found.

And now, having located the research literature, we shall turn our attention to how to read a research report. Especially we shall look at some of the critical skills and attitudes that readers need to develop if they are to read research skilfully and understand it thoroughly.

But first, we shall apply some of the preceding discussion practically.

— —

Practical Application of the Preceding Discussion

Project 1. You should get acquainted with some of the resources that we have mentioned in this chapter. Go to a library to explore the following:

1. *An index. Find any of the indexes mentioned on pages 23–24. Spend some time looking through the index, getting acquainted with the type of information it contains.*

2. *A bibliography. If your library has the Bibliographic Index, explore it. Check the card catalog to see if the library owns Besterman, Bibliography of Bibliographies.*

3. *Abstracts. Get acquainted with the abstracts mentioned on page 24. Check the card catalog to see if your library has any of the abstracts other than those mentioned in your text, or any others relating especially to your field of interest.*

4. *Reviews of research. A number of journals are devoted to reviewing research in specific fields. Of these the Review of Educational Research is, perhaps, more widely available than some of the others. In any event, go to the card catalog or the card file to the holdings in the periodicals room to see what review of research journals your library has. Inspect one or more of these. It is the role of these journals to discuss trends, recent developments, or current research in a particular field.*

Project 2. If your library is a large city library, a specialized professional library, or a university library, it may subscribe to one or more of the computer search services, such as ERIC or MEDLARS. If it does, go to the librarian in charge of this service and investigate how you can use it to find research studies on a particular subject.

If your library does not subscribe to such a service, write to the National Bureau of Standards, United States Department of Commerce, Washington, D.C. 20234, requesting publication NBSIR 78-1577, Diane Cunningham, Data Bases Available at the National Bureau of Standards Library, March, 1979. The list will also indicate the producer of hard copy for the particular data base listed.

Project 3. We discussed earlier in this chapter that frequently significant research reporting reaches us through the columns of the newspaper or news magazine. Make a collection of these. If the source is given—as it was in the stress-and-cancer release—see if you can find the report itself. Consult an index to see if you can locate the journal originally reporting the research. Compare the original report with that of the news release. On pages 16-21, we have discussed the nine constituent parts of a report. If you can find the research report, if not, use the newspaper or magazine release, and identify—as we did on page 23—as many of the nine component parts of a report as you can. If you wish to photocopy the report, then you might make the identification of as many of the nine parts of a report as you can, writing them in the margin opposite the place where that feature occurs. (See pages 30-32.)

HOW TO READ A RESEARCH REPORT

The items that we have outlined on pages 16-21 are the standard components of most research reports. Each scholarly journal, however, may have its own format for report organization. In reading a research report, therefore, the once-over-lightly treatment will give you an overview of the total organization of the study. This should be done before you attempt to read the report as a whole. Guidelines for reading any report may be stated briefly.

1. Read the title.
2. Read the abstract or summary.
3. Thumb through the report quickly, noting the main headings and subheadings, to get the organization of the report as a whole.
4. Go back to the beginning. Reading the report carefully and in detail, noting the problem which was researched and the manner in which the data were collected and interpreted. Note exactly what the researcher has written. What you read may not agree with your own thinking. No matter! Do not interpolate your own thoughts; do not infer anything more than is expressed on the page. In *reading* research, you have one responsibility: to *know precisely* what the *researcher* has said, and this must be uncolored by your own wishes, desires, preferences, or ideas.
5. Finally, read the conclusions. Then read again the problem. The conclusions should follow logically from the statement of the problem. The one should complement the other.

At this point, let us take a brief report and read it as we have suggested in the guidelines.

Journal of Counseling Psychology
1979, Vol. 26, No. 4, 352–354

1. Read the title thoughtfully.

2. Read the abstract. Here is a bird's—eye—view of the report.

3. Paragraphs 1–3: The introduction.
Background, rationale, and related studies are all mentioned in the opening remarks contained in these three paragraphs.

4. The statement of the research goal, or the problem, begins with the words: "Of particular interest in the present study. . . ." Phrased as a question it is: How appropriate were the responses of the volunteers as a professionally desirable criterion?

5. The related research studies (Carkhuff, Goodman and Dooley, etc.) are cited at appropriate points where these studies could contribute to the present study in either corollary research or in providing procedural techniques.

6. The method and design of the research is indicated under the heading of "Method." The characteristics of the subjects employed in the research is first described, then the procedures for securing the data are outlined. This obviously was a survey type of research design.

Brief Reports

On the Tendency for Volunteer Helpers to Give Advice

Don Knowles
University of Victoria, Victoria, Canada

The responses of volunteers to a telephone crisis line were evaluated to determine the presence of appropriate types of statements to offer to a caller during the initial phase of a call. Sample responses were drawn from 350 male and female volunteers to the community crisis-line service. Subjects ranged in age from 18 to 65 years and had a wide range of educational and occupational experiences. The study followed a descriptive model; random selections of 30 tape-recorded responses to each of 12 simulated calls were drawn and analyzed using the scoring system reported by Whalen and Flowers. At least 70% of the responses were advisements. The average proportion of advisements was particularly high for calls dealing with the areas of loneliness and dating. Feelings expressed by the callers were ignored by most of the volunteers. This pattern of many advisements and few reflections was considered inappropriate for the goals of most helping agencies. Implications for selection and training of volunteers were developed.

Data collected over a 3-year period from volunteers to a telephone crisis-line service were considered in the present study. Of particular interest was the quality of helping-intended responses given by volunteers when they first arrived at the agency. The expectation of providing help to callers may be so pronounced that the agency's goals of wanting the caller to feel respected and understood are jeopardized.

One difficulty arises when assistance is given in a manner which implies incompetence on the part of the recipient, thereby producing feelings of being a failure and resentment toward both the help and the person who provided it (Berkowitz & Connor, 1966). Further, overly ambitious offers of assistance convey a lack of respect for the recipient's ability to meet the demands of a situation (Carkhuff, 1969). The recipient may also interpret the assistance to mean that his or her own feelings and experiences are not important.

The development of *response mode categories* by Goodman and Dooley (1976) provided a framework for studying the type of communication offered in crisis-line conversations and counseling interviews. Six basic response categories have been identified: question, advisement, silence, interpretation, reflection, and self-disclosure. Of particular interest in the present study were advisements, an appropriate type of response for eliciting well-defined behavior but ineffective in eliciting rapport or encouraging self-exploration. What was being sought in responses of volunteers to the initial phase of a call was a high proportion of reflection statements and a low proportion of advisement statements.

Method

Subjects

Volunteer applicants to a community telephone crisis-line service were required to complete an application form, respond to simulated telephone calls, and participate in a brief interview. Ages ranged from 18 years to 65 years; level of education ranged from Grade 8 to postgraduate degree. About twice as many women as men applied. A wide variety of occupations were represented including clerical workers, students, housewives, receptionists, civil servants, and sales personnel. Most applicants had some related volunteer experience, but few had undertaken

This study was supported by a Faculty Research Grant from the University of Victoria. The assistance of Margaret McHugh in establishing the screening procedure and of Mackenzie Brooks and Chris Haugland in analyzing the data is acknowledged.
Requests for reprints should be sent to Don Knowles, Faculty of Education, University of Victoria, P.O. Box 1700, Victoria, British Columbia, Canada V8W 2Y2.

352

Reprinted by permission of the *Journal of Counseling Psychology* and also the author.

---

*These numbers refer to the corresponding numbered items in a research report, pp. 16–21.

extended training in areas related to the work of the telephone service. Responses were sampled, as described below, from those provided by 350 applicants to the service.

Procedure

Each applicant was presented with a series of five simulated calls which dealt with loneliness, child-parent relationships, drug use, dating, and locating accommodation and food. The statements were tape-recorded, following the general procedure reported by Carkhuff (1969, pp. 114-123). The statement presented some factual content and a relatively clear indication of the feelings of the speaker. For example, one of the loneliness calls had a young woman say the following:

Hello. I'm rattling around the house with just

little kids to talk to. My husband isn't home much and it's been ages since I've talked with another adult. The kids are pretty good but I get tired of no one but kids. I wish I could think of a way to get out of the house.

The statements concluded either with a declaration of what was troubling the caller or with a question about how the caller could "figure out what to do" or what the helper thought of the situation.

The calls were presented on a tape recorder; responses were recorded on a second tape recorder. The applicant was instructed to listen carefully to each call and "respond as you would if the caller was seeking your assistance in a time of some distress to him." A random selection of 30 responses to each call was drawn. The five areas of concern were represented by 12 different calls.

Table 1
Average Proportion of Responses in Each Response Mode Category for Male and Female Volunteers

Area of call	Sex	N	Reflect	Inter-pret	Advise	Ques-tion	Self-disclose	Other	Not scoreable
Loneliness									
Older woman	M	7	00	00	88	03	01	00	07
	F	17	02	01	85	09	02	00	00
Housewife	M	15	03	00	85	10	01	00	00
	F	15	06	00	79	06	07	01	00
Child-parent									
Dating daughter	M	12	00	00	76	12	11	00	00
	F	18	01	01	81	03	11	01	01
Talking	M	9	00	00	89	02	10	00	00
	F	21	00	00	87	08	04	00	02
Tense mother	M	13	07	00	75	11	03	00	04
	F	14	13	00	71	12	02	00	01
Drugs									
Try pot	M	14	09	01	79	04	04	00	02
	F	15	05	01	73	08	11	01	00
Brain change	M	12	04	00	77	13	02	01	02
	F	18	03	00	78	07	03	09	00
Woozy pills	M	11	00	00	91	09	00	00	00
	F	19	01	00	93	05	00	00	00
Dating									
Overweight	M	11	04	00	91	00	01	01	02
	F	19	00	00	94	02	04	00	00
Pregnant	M	16	03	01	86	08	01	00	00
	F	14	06	00	86	01	03	03	00
Accommodation									
Wanderer	M	10	01	00	82	07	00	00	10
	F	20	05	01	85	02	00	00	07
No welfare	M	11	00	00	86	02	00	00	03
	F	19	04	00	80	04	01	01	11

Note. Decimal points have been omitted. M = male; F = female.

After a description of the manner in which the research was structured (using the models of Carkhuff and Goodman and Dooley) the researcher then presents the data in tabular form.

Note that the figures given in this table are percentages. The response mode categories are those suggested by the research of Goodman and Dooley (See 13 of the introduction.)

The sex refers to the sex of the volunteer. The column headed "N" reports the number of volunteers responding to each area of call. N is a symbol that always means "Number of."

Chapter 4 in this text will provide some hints for reading of graphs, tables, and other devices for the presentation of data.

To this point in the study we have been introduced to the problematical situation, we have had the problem stated, the researcher has indicated the other research studies that have been of assistance in effecting this study, the procedure has been outlined by which the study was carried on, and the data obtained have been presented in tabular form. We are now ready for the researcher to indicate what all this means. What are the results of the study?

At this point in the report, the researcher describes the method by which he evaluated the responses. This section describes how the researcher extracted meaning from the data. To assist in this process he relied upon "the scoring system reported by Whalen and Flowers and the judgments of three independent judges."

The responses were scored by a graduate student, and then this evaluation was compared with the judging (scoring) of the same responses by a panel of judges.

7. What are the results? The researcher brings them all together in the paragraph entitled "Results."

8. In the "Discussion" the researcher presents his conclusions. From a professional counseling standpoint, the "high proportion of advisements" (the great amount of advice) was inappropriate. Now follow some suggestions for improving the situation. Finally, the research attempts to determine why the volunteers responded as they did. He theorizes that popular press "advice columns" may have had some influence.

9. The notes and references give the documentation for the studies cited in the report, should the reader wish to consult these sources.

Measure

The scoring system reported by Whalen and Flowers (1977), based on the response modes described by Goodman and Dooley (1976), was employed. Whalen and Flowers (1977) reported interjudge reliability coefficients ranging from .71 to 1.00, with most correlations in excess of .85, for the 12 categories with sufficient frequencies to permit computations. Scoring was conducted by a graduate student in counseling psychology. Each applicant's response was divided into components, defined as relatively complete thoughts which were separated from other components by change in voice tone or by silence, and assigned to a category. Proportions of total responses in each category were computed for each applicant. Interjudge agreement between the original scoring and that provided by three independent judges was 75%, for a sample of 60 responses, for advisements and reflections.

Results

The volunteers who responded to the simulated crisis-line calls in this study gave advice most of the time. As reported in Table 1, the advisement category accounted for an average of at least 70% of the responses. For the loneliness and dating calls in particular, the average proportion was closer to 90% in the advisement category. The average proportion of calls in the advisement category far surpassed the proportion in other categories for each of the 12 calls. In fact, at least one third of the volunteers gave all advisement responses to each call, ranging from 9 of 29 for the *try pot* call to 22 of 30 for the *overweight* call and 23 of 30 for the *woozy pills* call. In marked contrast were the small proportions of reflective responses, which ranged from 0% to 9% of total responses.

Discussion

The high proportion of advisements given by the majority of volunteers is considered inappropriate for the task they were provided. It seems unlikely that a caller hearing this advice would develop feelings of having been heard and respected. It would be advisable, therefore, to ensure that applicants to voluntary services are carefully screened and trained. An important contribution of training programs would be an expansion of the types of response modes available and the development of an understanding of the functions served by each mode. Goodman and Dooley (1976) have recommended that such training follow the increasing levels of difficulty of the modes: question, advisement, silence, interpretation, reflection, and self-disclosure.

The general results indicate that many volunteers equated the act of helping with the providing of advice. They appeared to want the caller to avoid feeling the pain or uneasiness that was being expressed. Others conveyed a tone that they were more knowledgeable than the caller, responding to the call as if it were a request for instruction. One could speculate that for many volunteers, the very directive responses appearing in popular press "advice columns" are salient sources about how best to offer assistance. Vigilance to this tendency of volunteer helpers seems warranted.

References

Berkowitz, L., & Connor, W. H. Success, failure, and social responsibility. *Journal of Personality and Social Psychology*, 1966, *4*, 664 669.

Carkhuff, R. R. *Helping and human relations: A primer for lay and professional helpers: Vol. 1. Selection and training.* Toronto: Holt, Rinehart & Winston, 1969.

Goodman, G., & Dooley, D. A framework for help-intended communication. *Psychotherapy*, 1976, *13*, 106–117.

Whalen, C. K., & Flowers, J. V. Effects of role and gender mix on verbal communication modes. *Journal of Counseling Psychology*, 1977, *24*, 281 287.

Received August 21, 1978 ∎

This is a brief report, and included here merely to give you some introduction to report reading. You should not, however, expect that every research report will follow this identical format. Those who report research do not necessarily have a standard format that they follow.

They do, however, broadly follow the guidelines and editorial preference of the journals in which the report is published. For example, here is the format used by two scholarly journals. They are arranged opposite each other so that you may compare likenesses and differences in each. In totality, they both add up to the common denominator of an acceptable format for reporting research findings. Each journal has its own editorial style. Expect to find some variation from journal to journal.

Format for Studies Published in *The Journal of Social Psychology*	Format for Studies Published in *The Journal of Negro Education*
Title	Title
Author	Author
Summary [Abstract]	Abstract
A. Introduction	[Introduction]
B. Method	A. Method
1. Subjects	1. Subjects and Procedure
2. Materials used	2. Instruments
3. Procedure	B. Results
C. Results	C. Conclusions
D. Discussion	
E. References	[The references in this journal are incorporated as footnotes at the bottom of the page on which the reference is made.]

Practical Application of the Preceding Discussion

Project 1. Using the suggestions for locating research reports on pages 21-28 of this chapter, find five research reports in a subject area of your interest. Then, applying the material presented on pages 15-21, analyze each of the reports with marginal comments, as has been done on pages 30-32. Perhaps you might do well to photocopy each report, noting your comments on an attached marginal strip, after the manner of pages 30-32. Do not attempt to explain the statistical aspects of the report. You will do this later.

Project 2. You will complete this project much later in this book: at the close of chapter 6. For that reason, file the reports which you have analyzed in Project 1. You will need these later to explain the statistical concepts found in them.

CHAPTER 4   The Language of Line and Column

What Is It?
How to Read It
How to Comprehend Its Meaning

Every research report relies upon two forms of communication: *verbal communication,* in which description and narration explain to the reader what the researcher has done and what results have been obtained; and *symbolic communication,* in which graphic representation, tabular array, or statistical values convey to the reader the factual data essential to the communication of the researcher's message.

The last chapter dealt with the research report as a form of verbal communication and outlined the skills necessary to read the report so that the consumer of research might comprehend the researcher's message accurately and clearly. In this chapter, we will discuss the reading skills necessary to comprehend symbolic communication: graphs, charts, tables, and similar non-verbal forms of data presentation.

In a research report, the researcher ought to present the data on which he has based his conclusions. This is usually done by summary tables, by graphs or charts. Behind every table, graph or chart may reside great masses of raw data in the form of responses that were gathered directly from the population of the study. The raw data may consist of answers to stacks of questionnaires, bundles of completed standardized tests, or pages upon pages of individual laboratory observations and notes, all of which are represented in the report by a few dots upon a grid or a column of figures in a table.

Since it is impracticable to reproduce in a report the considerable quantity of raw data which every researcher collects, we must be content to have such voluminous body of fact reduced to a dot on a graph, a numerical value in a table or a statistical value.

Occasionally, however, when the primary data are of such singular importance as to warrant their presence in the report, the full reproduction of them may be included, usually as an appendix to the report proper. So doing makes such data available to any who may want to retrace the researcher's steps and to confirm the conclusions or interpretations given those data in the body of the report.

Such full presentation is given at times in doctoral dissertations or in other reports where the data may be of supreme importance in evaluating the validity of the conclusions or in determining the quality of the research. Such inclusion may, of course, create a report which may be voluminous and unwieldy. For this reason, we generally dispense with a full presentation of the data and present instead only a summarization of it in tables or graphs.

Nearly always what appears on a chart or a graph is but the tip of the data iceberg, but that tip can be highly significant for those who know how to appraise and appreciate it.

GRAPHS

Two kinds of people look at paintings: those who merely look at the picture, and those who view the painting appreciatively as a work of art. Two kinds of people, likewise, look at graphs: those who merely see a line or lines imposed upon a grid, and those who see with insight what lies *beyond* the superimposed line and by so doing comprehend the significance of the total presentation.

For, per square inch, graphs pack more information upon the page than any other device that presents raw data in visual form. How, then, do you look at a graph? Here are some simple guidelines.

Begin with the grid. The study of any graph begins with the *grid* or *matrix. A grid is a series of lines, crossing at right angles to each other at the intersection of which, or at any point between the intersections, data are located.* These lines are called *coordinates.* The left-hand marginal line of the grid is the *vertical axis* and is referred to as the *ordinate.* The bottom line of the grid is the *horizontal axis*, and is called the *abscissa.* These are the two principal axes of any graph, and along them is arranged a series of values. Thus, upon a grid we have two factors whose values are represented: the factor whose *strength* is scaled on the ordinate, and the second factor, whose dynamic is indicated on the abscissa. Think of these two factors as forces, each acting upon the other at the several points where they cross at right angles within the grid.

To make this concept clear, here is a simple graph, representing the germination and growth of an ordinary bean.

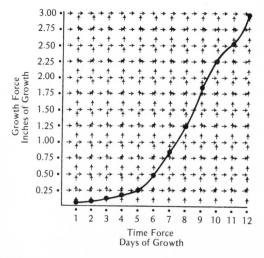

GERMINATION AND GROWTH OF AN ORDINARY BEAN

The grid, therefore, is a dynamic *field of interacting forces*. On the one hand, we have the *growth force*; on the other, the *time force*. The grid is the field where the action takes place for the germinating bean. Both forces are powerful, irresistible. Anyone who has ever planted a row of beans recognizes this. Prodded by moisture and warmth, the growth force within the bean soon drives down into the soil the rudimentary taproot. Then, spreading its cotyledons, the bean pushes up the mass of earth that overlays it and emerges from below the surface of the soil. So much for the growth force.

Time is an equally unrelenting force. The development of the bean is a function of both time *and* growth; for growth is a time-consuming process. The bean is cast into the row and covered with earth. Time passes. The root emerges. More time passes. The stalk grows, and after a time, two tiny "wings"—the cotyledons of the bean—break through the surface of the soil. And all this, the graph expresses with a single bold expressive line! And beneath the line is the play of elemental forces, represented by the arrows emanating from each factor and interacting in a complex matrix. Every grid is, therefore, a crosshatch of dynamics—a "field" where lines of force stream inward and upward from each axis, thus catching any data that are superimposed on it in a crossfire of influences.

Graphs are not static representations. They are dramatic portrayals of a complex and dynamic interaction that is at work upon any data depicted upon their crossed lines.

If you think of graphical presentations in this manner, it will help you to understand the essential character of the data presented. Each point on a graph line is, thus, a co-relation of determinants; and to read a graph adequately, we must never lose sight of this fact.

Study the configuration of the line. The line on the grid is profoundly expressive. To those who look insightfully, the configuration of the line reveals much that the untrained eye fails to see. How, then, does one acquire this insightfulness? To answer that question, we must penetrate the barrier of lines and grids, and all the paraphernalia of graphical representation and see clearly the arena where occur the everyday events of real life. One basic axiom forms the bedrock upon which research, upon which statistics, upon which graphical presentation of data all rest: *The facts of the real world dictate what is and what is not possible in research procedures, in portrayal of data, or in presenting facts by graphic or statistical means.*

With graphs especially, *what is, is the way it is because life is the way it is.* The next few paragraphs will explain that statement.

The events of the real world happen in four principal ways:

1. They happen in terms of a growth or decay phenomenon.
2. They happen in an accelerative and then a decelerative—a crescendo–diminuendo—sequence.
3. They happen arrhythmically, unpredictably, and irregularly.
4. They happen with great imbalance or with abnormal amplitude in one sector of the system which is atypical for all the rest of the system.

Each of these events traces unmistakable configurations on a grid. Hence, a glance at the line configuration indicates the type of event that gave rise to it. We shall discuss each of the situations we have outlined above and illustrate these with hypothetical graph configuration patterns.

Growth. The first of the configurations, we have already discussed. It is the characteristic *S* curve, sometimes called the Gompertz curve, or the Pearl-Reed curve. We saw it above in part in the example of the bean. Growth has special characteristics. Whether it be a bean, a human being, or an urban community, the pattern of its growth and development projects the same general configuration on a grid. Growth begins simply and at a rate of low acceleration. With the bean, it begins with a mysterious "germination" between the cotyledons. With the human or animal individual, it originates with two microscopic cells. With the urban community, with perhaps a crossroads and a half-dozen houses. For a short period, the phenomenon of growth progresses slowly. Then comes the growth spurt. Growth is described mathematically as a geometric progression. But growth has another characteristic: growth units multiply to a certain point geometrically, then a slowing down begins, and finally growth stops. That is the point that we call *maturity*. Beans do not keep growing until they reach the clouds, nor children until they look down on skyscrapers! Eventually, the growth process levels off and finally, perhaps, even a slight decline.

Remember how you grew? You were a little boy or girl until about eight or ten years of age, within a few years, you shot up to full stature of adult maturity. All growing things follow that pattern.

There is a waiting time after the bean is dropped into the furrow. Then the gentle break-through. Comes the spurt: you can almost *see* it grow. Within a few weeks, it becomes a mature plant; growth stops. The process is complete.

All the dynamics, all the mystery of growth is expressed in one exquisitely eloquent curve—the curve of the growth phenomenon. And it is one of the four curve types that you will find in research reports.

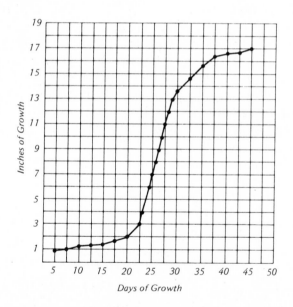

GERMINATION AND GROWTH RATE OF A BEAN

The normal curve. We come now to a second curvilinear configuration.[1] The shape of the curve is distinctive; the data that it expresses are common to a broad spectrum of life's happenings. The pattern of these events is on this model: they begin with a few instances, these gradually increase until a maximum frequency of occurrences happens. This climax

_____
[1] See page 37, (2).

of occurrences generally happens about midway along the range of events. Then, the frequency of events drops away until, as at the beginning, only a few occurrences occur at the other end of the activity range.

The curve that describes such phenomena—quite unlike the growth curve—has a characteristic shape which is perhaps better known than that of any other graphical configuration. It is in the shape of a bell, hence we call it the *bell curve*, the *normal curve*, or the *Gaussian curve*, because of its association with Karl Friedrich Gauss, a German mathematician (1777–1855).

Thousands of daily happenings are depicted by the normal curve. Take any main highway leading out of a large city. On a normal day the traffic flow will usually follow a bell-shaped pattern. Let's begin with traffic activity at two o'clock in the afternoon. Ten cars per minute pass a given point. By three o'clock, the number has increased: school buses have been added to the traffic flow, housewives bringing children from school or coming home from afternoon events. By four o'clock, the early office departure adds to the rising stream of vehicles. Five o'clock sees the peak of commuters with all lanes jammed. By six, the highway activity begins to subside. At seven, couples go out for the evening, but the road is fairly clear. Eight o'clock finds about ten cars per minute passing the observer—the pattern as it was at two o'clock in the afternoon.

Now, let's graph that on a grid.

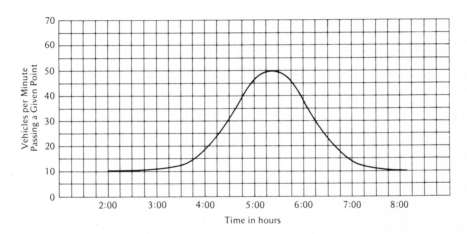

RUSH HOUR TRAFFIC ILLUSTRATES THE NORMAL CURVE DISTRIBUTION

What we have observed on the highway is a pattern that we shall see repeatedly in events which take place around us: people arriving for a football game, or at the theater. There are the early arrivals, then the number of those arriving builds steadily to a climax just before game or curtain time. Then the arrivals subside until a few stragglers form a latecomers counterpart of the early arrivals at the other end of the activity pattern. Further evidence of Gaussian curve application is seen by noting the number of inches of snow that fall from October to March in a northern state, the scores on a general information test taken by a random group of people selected at random from those who pass a certain downtown street corner at a given time on any given day. Plot any of these data, and you will have a configuration reasonably resembling the normal distribution curve. We could go on and on. We may almost say that the normal curve is the curve of everyday events.

Whimsicality and unpredictability. In the third category of events[2] with characteristic graph profiles are those phenomena evidencing capricious, irregular, unpredictable, or erratic behavior. Normal curve behavior we can reasonably predict, and statisticians employ it for precisely that purpose. The curve that we are about to describe, no one can predict. It is the result of the pure whimsicality of nature.

Take a hurricane. We have an anemometer to record the wind velocity during the passage of the storm. When we look at the graph after the storm, we find an erratic curve, unpredictable, with its zig-zag dips and peaks, and uneventful plateaus. It is a picture of the capriciousness of the wind. At one instant, the wind blew violently; then it dropped off; then, rose slightly; then, died almost to a calm; another gust, shot up to the velocity of hurricane force, and so on and on. The profile of the graph is asymmetrical and resembles nothing in common with the other two configurations which we have described earlier.

Graph the speed of an automobile traveling from downtown in one city to downtown in another city 25 miles away. The graph line will look almost like the hurricane profile. Plotted against a time scale, there will be times when you may encounter a stop sign and your speed may approach zero, but, then, you may attain speeds varying from five or ten miles per hour to 55 miles an hour on a throughway. And even there, your speed will vary depending on slower-moving vehicles ahead of you and your inability to pass. For storm or speedometer, a characteristic graph may look like the following:

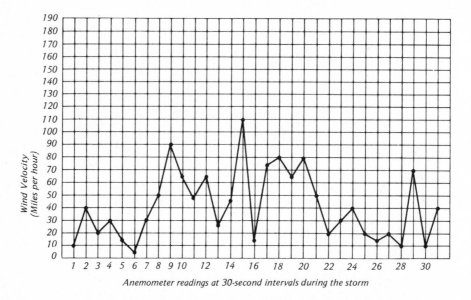

RECORD OF WIND VELOCITY DURING A HURRICANE

Inequality. Finally, we have the graph of inequality—gross inequality. Some statisticians and researchers may call this merely a skewed normal curve, but when it becomes so abnormal as to have a characteristic profile, it may be well to consider it a type of its own. It represents a situation that may happen indeed in everyday life.[3]

---

[2] See page 37, (3).
[3] See page 37, (4).

Take an example: a town mining silica sand for a glass works has a resident population of 500 families. The heads of the families work in the mines. There is, however, the mine-owning company which is composed of four officers and a mine superintendent. The officers live in spacious homes in a small town five miles away from the mining community. We are interested in the *average* annual salary of all of the employees of this company. The W-2 Forms sent by the company to the Internal Revenue Service might report salaries such as these:

President, Silica Sand and Glass Co.	$ 675,000.00
Vice president, Silica Sand and Glass Co.	325,000.00
Secretary, Silica Sand and Glass Co.	300,000.00
Treasurer, Silica Sand and Glass Co.	275,000.00
Superintendent of the mine, Silica S. & G. Co.	100,000.00
Miners, 500 total, each	10,000.00
Total annual company payroll, officers of the company	1,675,000.00
Total annual payroll, miners	5,000,000.00
Average salary of officers (1,675,000.00 ÷ 5)	335,000.00
Average salary of miners	10,000.00

Commit this data to a graph, and it will show a configuration totally unlike any of the others we have presented.

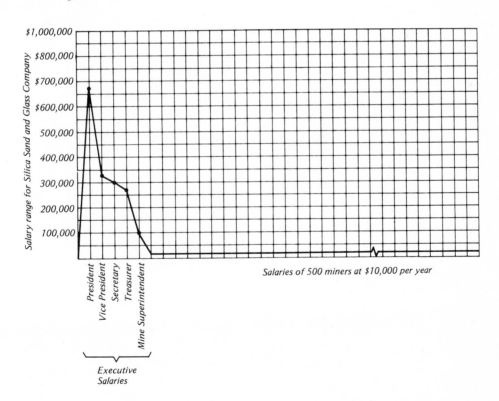

EARNINGS OF THE EMPLOYEES OF THE SILICA SAND AND GLASS COMPANY

We have, of course, presented *idealized* situations. The graphs that you will inspect in most research reports will not show such perfection of contour, but in broad configuration they will resemble to a greater or lesser degree one of the four foregoing types. This observation brings us to the third guideline for reading graphs. We are dealing now with practicality. The graphs that we shall examine in research reports demand other skills which we shall now discuss.

Read the captions and the legend carefully. In research reports, graphs have captions. These advise the reader what message the graph is attempting to convey. The graph on page 36 has been entitled "The Germination and Growth of an Ordinary Bean."

Captions also frequently indicate the specific units in which the data charted upon the graph is calibrated. This is sometimes expressed by the addition of such phrases as "in percent," "in millions of dollars," "in centimeters." We have captioned the graph on page 38: "Germination and Growth of a Bean." This, together with the two legends, one showing the days of growth and the other the inches of growth, gives full information for the reading of the graph.

Frequently also in connection with a graphical presentation you may find another feature, the *legend*. The legend is a short explanation of the meaning of the various line configurations presented on the grid, or of any symbols that may be employed for special designation of certain data. If, for example, we wish to plot two presentations on one grid, one of these may be a solid line, the other, a dotted line. Three designations may be represented as (1) a solid line for one kind of data, (2) a dotted line for the second type of data, and (3) a broken line for the third variety of data. These may all be plotted on the same grid, with the same calibrations on the axes. Here is a graph with *eight* lines, indicating causes of fatalities resulting from human-caused events.

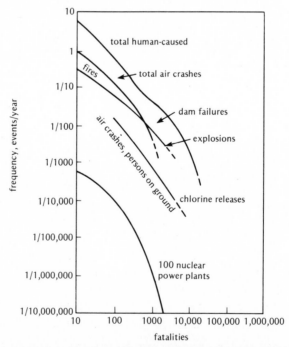

ESTIMATED FREQUENCY OF FATALITIES DUE TO HUMAN-CAUSED EVENTS (From McGraw-Hill Encyclopedia of Energy, Daniel N. Lapedes, Editor, page 488. New York: McGraw-Hill Book Company, 1976. Reprinted by permission.)

Inspect carefully the intervals on each axis. Do not trust your first impression when looking at graphs. Graphs can be misleading and convey an entirely wrong impression at first glance. You must study them carefully. How large are the gradations on each of the axes? Do they proceed in equidistant intervals? Generally, the size of the interval will alter the shape of the configuration. Curves that sweep dramatically upward are usually the result of decreased interval size. They are attention-getting. Compare the one below with the other which scarcely gets off the baseline. Which captures the attention at first sight?

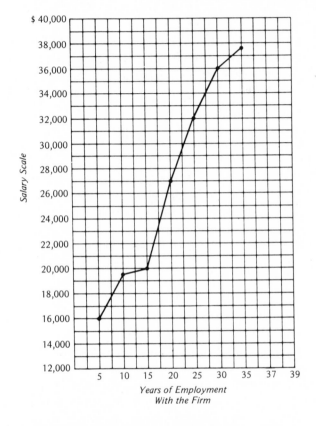

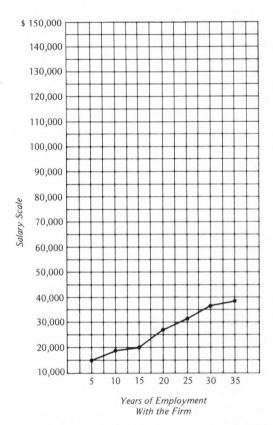

SALARY RECORD OF AN EMPLOYEE WITH THE ABC CORPORATION (GRAPH 1)

SALARY RECORD OF AN EMPLOYEE WITH THE ABC CORPORATION (GRAPH 2)

If you inspected those graphs carefully, you would see that they both present the same information. Yet one commands attention, where the other is unpretentious. Both have their function as instruments of communication, but while the second speaks to you *sotto voce,* the first screams at you with an ever higher and higher pitch. The trick has been of course, to change the interval on the vertical axis. In graph 1, the salary scale proceeds at $2,000 intervals; in graph 2, it jumps $10,000 at a time.

As the size of the interval on either axis is reduced, the line plotting the data will become more dramatic. It will reveal in magnified form the influences which have been at work upon or within the data. Sometimes it is highly desirable for us to see this. That's the purpose of microscopes in the laboratory: to magnify the object of study so that you may see it in more meaningful detail. Whether you are studying microorganisms or data, sometimes the magnified view is good. Graph 1 is magnification; graph 2, miniaturization. Look through the wrong end of a telescope. Details are submerged in the overall broad view of the data.

The point we are here making is, if you are to read research and understand it, then you must be aware of what graphical presentation is capable of doing. You should appraise carefully the data the researcher has plotted, always with an awareness that what is taking place upon the grid has been directly influenced by the values on the axes.

Look well, then, to the information expressed on the ordinate and the abscissa before making any judgments with respect to the data plotted on the grid.

Study carefully the "peaks" and "valleys" of the curve. Every peak, every valley in the contour of graphed data is significant. The line peaks, or the line dips because of some influence, or a series of influences, which have operated upon the data. The *explanation* of the peaks and valleys is properly the obligation of the researcher. Those who read research, therefore, may reasonably expect that the researcher will offer some explanation for any unexpected behavior of the graphed line. Careful researchers should inspect their data with meticulous attention, pointing out any possible causes for atypical line behavior, and in reading research you should expect graphs to be explained and tables to be analyzed.

For the next several pages we will illustrate how a graph may be analyzed, and what we mean by atypical behavior. Our purpose in doing this is twofold: (1) to illustrate the comments made above and to demonstrate how peaks and valleys may alert us to significant facts that may lie below the graphed line; and (2) to anticipate at this point the interpretation of a historical graph. The last chapter of this book will be devoted to a discussion of historical research, but in connection with this chapter, the discussion here of the historical graph seems entirely appropriate. A somewhat extended discussion, therefore, will follow, illustrating, as it does, some matters already presented in this chapter and anticipating the discussion of historical research in Chapter 7.

Here is a graphical representation of the growth of the population of Spain from the year 400 B.C. to 1975 A.D. with an extrapolated projection to the year 2000.[4]

At the opening of this section on the discussion of graphs, we indicated that those who comprehend the message of a graph often "see with insight what lies beyond the superimposed line." That is the way we shall attempt to analyze the graph above. We begin with a basic principle: A nation's population is a function of a nation's history. You cannot study one without knowledge of the other. We shall study this graph by applying some of the guidelines mentioned earlier in this chapter.

Study the grid. Examine the incremental units upon its axes. The vertical axis indicates the size of the population; the horizontal axis, the time span. But look closely. Whereas the vertical scale progresses in uniform increments of 1,000,000 population for each unit on the axis, the horizontal axis shows no such symmetry. From 400 B.C. to 1000 A.D., the scale is in units of 200 years each; from 1000 to 1500, the time interval is one-half that of the previous scale—in 100 year increments; but from 1500 to 2000 A.D. halving again takes place—each unit represents a span of only 50 years. Although the grid spaces are uniform, the scalar values of the last 500 years are only one-fourth of those of the first 1400 years.

This altering of the scale on the horizontal axis presents a false graphical impression. The time interval shrinks progressively despite the fact that the grid distance remains constant.

---

[4] Colin McEvedy and Richard Jones, *Atlas of World Population History*, Penguin Reference Books series, New York: Penguin Books, 1978, p. 101.

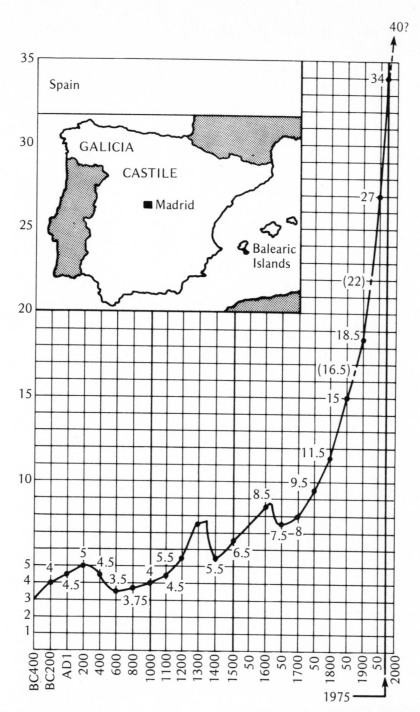

GROWTH OF SPANISH POPULATION: 400 B.C. TO 1975 A.D. (With extrapolated projection to 2000 A.D.)

If, therefore, we are to get a true picture of the population fluctuation we must rescale the graph on its horizontal axis. We may do this in two ways: either keeping a consistency of 50 year intervals for the entire span of 2400 years, or plotting it on a uniform scale of

200 year units for the same period. First, the data plotted on a uniform scale of 50-year units will appear like this.

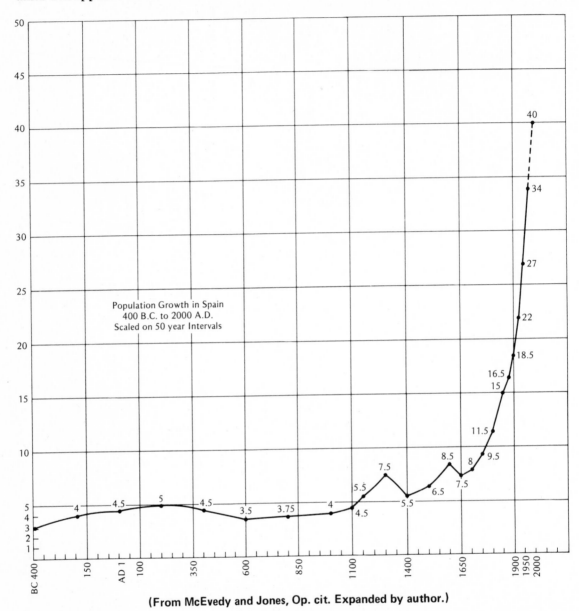

Population Growth in Spain
400 B.C. to 2000 A.D.
Scaled on 50 year Intervals

(From McEvedy and Jones, Op. cit. Expanded by author.)

How different the message now! In the 2400-year span of Spain's population history, the nation hovered for more than 1200 years—half the entire historical span—with a population between 3,000,000 and 5,000,000. Growth was gradual and undulating. Then from 1200 to 1800 A.D. peaks the valleys of population growth appeared. The band of fluctuation was somewhat broader. Instead of rising and falling between 3,000,000 and 5,000,000, the population for the next 600 years rose and subsided, rose and subsided, and then rose again between 5,000,000 and 10,000,000 people in the nation. It has been only within the last 200 years that the population boom has been compelling and dramatic. Between 1750 and 1800 the population figure crossed the 10,000,000 line. From then on, the swoop upward has been steep and relentless.

Compare the graph on page 45 with that on page 46. It conveys an entirely different message. The graph that we have just presented has presented Spain's population growth in slow motion—in 50-year time frames. Suppose we run the record at a faster rate—on a time-span of 200 years to the frame. The *total visual impression* will be entirely different. Look at the graph below. How striking! Here the impression is one of compression and rocket-like ascent. In this featuring of the data, the slow undulation of 1600 years is entirely wiped out and we see a peak, a valley, and a brief plateau from which the population growth is launched into an almost vertical trajectory.

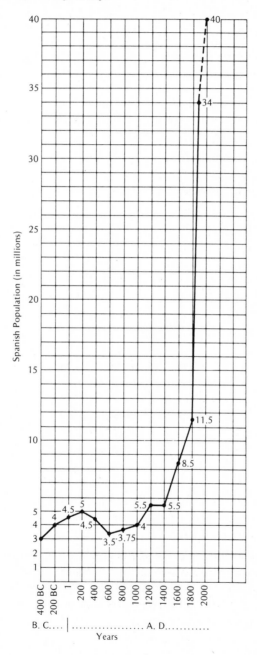

SPANISH POPULATION GROWTH 400 B.C. TO 200 A.D. IN 200-YEAR INTERVALS (From McEvedy and Jones, Op. cit. Scale condensed by author.)

This presentation of the data seems to suggest that the population growth took off about 1400 A.D. and has zoomed unswervingly upward ever since. The fluctuation shown in the 50-year graph between 1400 and 1700 is lost in this 200-year scale, and it would seem to suggest that the population spurt began 250 years earlier than that shown in the 50-year graph.

You may now be able to appreciate the words you read earlier: "Do not trust your first impression when looking at graphs. Graphs can be misleading and convey an entirely wrong impression at first glance. You must study them carefully." Graphs, while they have their value in presenting data in a dramatic visual form, also have their limitations. They are but *one* way in which the researcher may present the data, and those who would read research and understand it must learn to read graphs with a questioning mind and an observing eye. And what we have done thus far has not required any other skills than those two.

However, we made one suggestion earlier that "a nation's population is a function of a nation's history." Graphs merely reflect the dynamics that reside within the facts, and when graphing the data shows unusual fluctuation of line, it usually indicates that influences have been at work of which the fluctuations are merely surface indications.

Nothing just happens. When there is wide fluctuation, the researcher should be alert to that fact and begin searching the data for the cause of the disturbance. The reader of research should also be in an interrogatory frame of mind and expect that the researcher will provide some explanation.

We began this discussion with the aim of analyzing in two ways the graph of the growth of the Spanish population (1) to illustrate the need to study a graph carefully and inspect the grid intervals closely as factors which may influence the message that the graph conveys, and (2) to observe how historical data can be presented in graphical form, and the problems involved in reading historical graphs.

We have already explored the first part of the overall goal. The material that we shall present in the next few pages will have close relevance to the presentation of graphical data in historical research; for, in reading research of this type, we must look behind the graphed line to the historical facts which have influenced its configuration. This we shall now do.

Earlier in this chapter we suggested that a nation's population phenomenon is a function of the nation's history. The 50-year graph, therefore, is a reflection of the longitudinal history of the Spanish people. To fully explain the graph we must look at the historical record. To understand the profile of the graph *from a historical standpoint*, we have inserted—at critical points—alphabetic symbols in a circle. This will help us to correlate the historical background with the 50-year graph.

The graph begins with Spain in 400 B.C. (A).[5] Now, in 400 B.C., Spain was a land on the western rim of the world. The civilized world of that time regarded Spain with about as much attention as we today give to Antarctica. Few people had ever gone to Spain. The world of the day was the world of the Eastern Mediterranean and of Asia Minor—the world of Greece and of Persia, of India and of China, far, far away. The great names in 400 B.C. were Xenophon and Artaxerxes, Sophocles, Euripides, and Socrates. In 399—one year after the date with which the chart begins, Socrates was put to death in Athens. That provides us with a reference point. By 200 B.C., Rome had become influential in the West, and some Romans had infiltrated the Iberian peninsula. With the growth of the empire, Rome ex-

---

[5] Letters in parentheses refer to the same letter designations on the graph following. Historical event and graph contour are thus synchronized.

panded into Gaul and Britain, into North Africa and into Spain. In consequence, Spain's population grew steadily. (B)

Beginning with the third century A.D., Rome experienced difficulties. At first the problems were economic; later, military. From the North, Germanic hoards swept into the Eternal City. The empire disintegrated. Population declined, especially in the provinces. (C). With the sixth century, the Germanic tribes pushed into Spain; and in the eighth century came the Arabs. Again, Spain's population curve turned upward. (D).

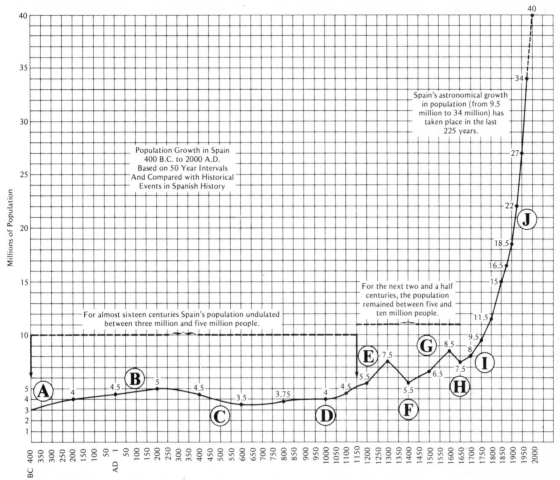

SPANISH POPULATION GROWTH CORRELATED WITH THE EVENTS IN SPANISH HISTORY (From McEvedy and Jones, Op. cit. Adapted and modified by the author.)

The medieval boom (E) was checked by the incursions of the Black Death, and between 1300 and 1400 it cut the Spanish population back to 5.5 million. (F)

World attention had shifted from the Eastern Mediterranean to the Atlantic. The age of exploration began. Commerce grew. Population in the countries of the western Mediterranean surged upward (G). But Spain's economic crisis in the early 17th century again caused the population to sag by a million—from 8.5 million in 1600 to 7.5 million in 1650. By the middle of the 18th century Spain's population was, for the fourth time, again on the rise. The country had fallen far behind its European neighbors. Recovery came slowly (I), but with the onset of the 19th century the final boom was on. (J) By 1975, there were 34,000,000 Spaniards in Spain alone. Demographers predict that another 6,000,000 will be added by century's end.

We probably have no need to comment further what the words mean with which this section on graphs was introduced: [those who truly read graphs] "see with insight what lies *beyond* the superimposed line and, by so doing, comprehend the significance of the total presentation."[6] We will have more to say about this in Chapter 7.

One final word should probably be said about a basic characteristic of the line graph. The graphs that we have just been studying afford a good example. Lines, by their very nature, suggest motion. This implies that line graphs can never be static representations. Our eyes follow the line, left to right, over undulations—a slight rise, an unexpected dip—and, then, the final powerful climb: the whole, suggestive of movement. The normal curve also suggests a sensation of graceful rise and gentle fall. And the growth curve begins gently, gains altitude rapidly and levels off in a sustained flight. Whatever the configuration, lines suggest motion: subdued, subjective, psychological motion, but, nevertheless, the subtle suggestion of ongoing events—of data in action.

There are, however, other devices for representing quantified data, and these we will now examine.

The bar graph. A modification of the line graph is the bar graph or *histogram*. Histograms and line graphs have much in common. Both are oriented to an axis-value system. Both are two-dimensional: vertical and horizontal. All who are acquainted with the histogram will recognize its characteristic shape immediately. It has either the "skyline" effect—that of taller and shorter buildings contiguous to each other—or the "shoreline" effect, in which bars jut out from the vertical axis to give an uneven vertical contour. In the histogram, the magnitude of the value is represented by the length of the bar. Conversion of line graph to histogram, or vice versa, is a very simple process as we shall illustrate in the following examples.

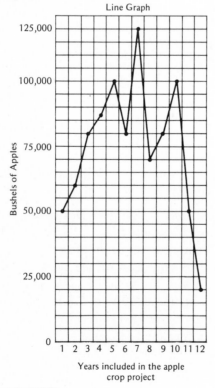

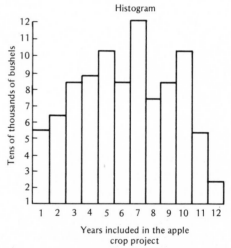

**APPLE CROP SURVEY:
YORK-ADAMS DISTRICT**

---

[6] See page 36.

Certainly, as we compare those two representations of the same data, we are aware of the difference in feeling that each gives the viewer. The line graph seems to be a much more agile type of presentation. The histogram is more massive. It probably is better suited to the expression of volume, of size, of mass. That is precisely the way we have used it here: to represent the *size* of the apple crop in the York-Adams district.

The three-dimensional histogram. The suggestion of mass is achieved by turning a histogram into a three-dimensional figure. The following from *The New York Times Index*[7] adequately illustrates the point:

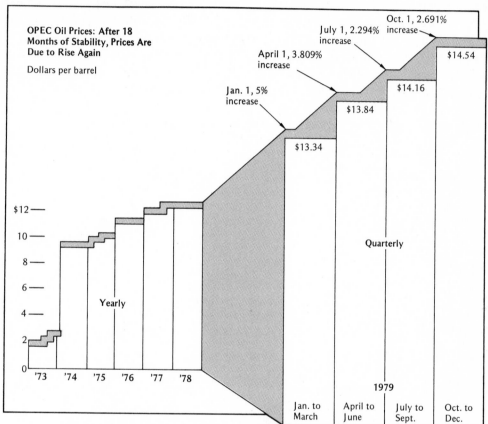

OPEC OIL PRICES IN THREE-DIMENSIONAL REPRESENTATION

The effect produced by the three-dimensional histogram graph is largely psychological. In the illustration above, the four quarterly slabs which are suddenly thrust forward seem to overpower the modest histogram in the background. That's what three-dimensionalism does.

The integrity of the three-dimensional graph is questionable because it distorts the representation of the data in order to dramatize it. What has been done in this graph is exactly what was done in the graph showing the growth of the population of Spain. The values on the axes have been changed. Try a few simple comparisons to see the degree of distortion that occurs when three-dimensionalism is employed. Compare, for instance the *width* of the yearly bars (in the background) with the *width* of the massive blocks for the four *quarters* of 1979. The total width of the base for 1979 exceeds by a quarter of an inch the total width of *all* the columns from 1973-1978. Again, lay a straight edge along the

------

[7]*The New York Times Index*, 1977, p. 1180.

51

horizontal *top* of the first quarter column for 1979 ($13.34). Project it to the left side of the graph. Note where it meets the left-hand margin. The difference between $12.00 and $13.34 is the same as the distance from 0 to $6 on the left-hand scale.

Those who read research should be highly suspicious of the more dramatic types of graphical representation. In a very subtle way, they introduce distortion into the presentation of the data which, without careful analysis upon the part of the research consumer, may convey a very erroneous message.

Pie graphs and pictographs. Pie graphs are common graphical devices for indicating a division of a totality. Financial institutions and corporations often make use of the pie graph in their corporate reports to indicate how moneys have been allocated or spent for various causes.

Usually, the sections of the pie graph are expressed in per cent ratios of the whole. The pie graph is a convenient visual device for showing a comparison between the several wedge-shaped areas and the totality of the whole.

Below are two pie graphs,[8] the upper one representing the relative areas of each of the continents to the total land area of the whole earth. The lower graph shows the relative size

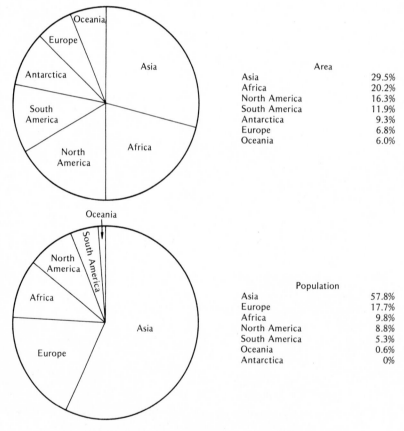

Area	
Asia	29.5%
Africa	20.2%
North America	16.3%
South America	11.9%
Antarctica	9.3%
Europe	6.8%
Oceania	6.0%

Population	
Asia	57.8%
Europe	17.7%
Africa	9.8%
North America	8.8%
South America	5.3%
Oceania	0.6%
Antarctica	0%

AREA AND POPULATION OF CONTINENTS

[8] From Victor Showers, *The World in Figures.* (New York: John Wiley, 1973), page 10.

of the population of each of the land areas. Compare the areas of Asia and Africa in the upper graph. There is not much difference in the size of these two areas geographically. Compare them in the lower graph with respect to the population of each. The disparity is overwhelming. Whereas Asia has only 9.3 percent more land area than Africa, it has 48 percent more people. Notice that the lower graph shows that Asia has more than half the population of the entire earth. That fact comes through in pie-graph representation more vividly than, perhaps, in any other form of presentation. Where the data is holistic, its presentation by means of pie-graph is probably most effective.

Here, it may be well to remark that each graphical device has its unique strengths and weaknesses. Each graphical representation has a particular function which it performs best. For example, data which arise out of a situation in which there is fundamentally the concept of motion—such as the "motion" of growth (as we saw it expressed in the growth of the bean and the growth of a nation's population) or the motion of fluctuation (such as that expressed in the Dow-Jones charting of the rise and fall of certain representative stocks, or of temperature or barometric pressure)--the line graph is perhaps the most effective graphical tool. Where the fundamental concept is that of mass or volume (as in the number of bushels— a volumetric measure—of apples), the histogram is perhaps more appropriate. Where the data represent a holistic situation, and the segments of that totality are shown as proportional parts, the pie graph presents such data best. And, since you wish to read and understand research, it is appropriate that you should appreciate the uniqueness of each specific graphical device to present a particular type of data most effectively.

The *pictograph* is another device, like the pie chart, to show proportional concepts. In the pictograph, however, a *picture* for the idea being presented is used and the magnitude of the various factors is shown by using the horizontal bar-graph technique. For example, we wish to show a comparison of the proportion of an industry's commodities which are transported by three separate types of carrier: railroads (suggested by a picture of a freight car), trucks, and airlines. Each symbol represents a certain number of units, such as 100,000 tons. We may have a graph that is similar to this.

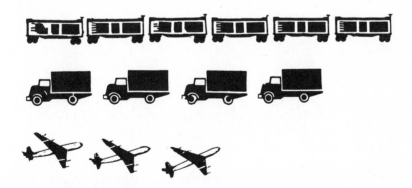

PROPORTION OF TRANSPORTATION BY THREE TYPES OF CARRIER

The pictograph is interesting and attention-getting. It is rarely employed in formal research reports. It is an extremely dramatic means of presenting data, and most researchers would consider it too garish to merit use in a research report.

CHARTS

Charts are graphic devices, employed to show a process, an overall organizational plan, or to convey a general idea comprising both function and organization. Charts are, thus, of three general types: the so-called *flow charts*, *organizational charts*, and *informational charts*. In research-report reading you will encounter all three of these types. We shall discuss each briefly.

A *flow chart* usually presents the progress of events through a system. An example is perhaps the best way to appreciate the function and purpose of the flow chart. In these days of energy consciousness, it may be well to inspect a flow-chart depicting the total energy

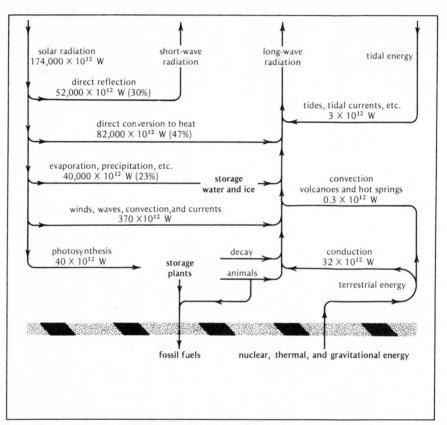

CYCLE OF EARTH ENERGY SOURCES. (From M. K. Hubbert, U.S. Energy Resources: A Review as of 1972, Part I, in A National Fuels and Energy Policy Study, U.S. Ninety-third Congress, Second session, Senate Committee on Interior and Insular Affairs, Series No. 93-40 (92-75), 1974. Washington, D.C. Government Printing Office. Reprinted from the public domain.)

system of the earth. It is essentially a description of our terrestrial sources of energy and how the cycle of the conservation of energy operates. Arrows indicate the input and out-flow of energy. Note that there are three input channels: solar radiation, tidal energy, and energy from the earth itself in the forms of nuclear, thermal and gravitational energy. Likewise the outflow of energy is also threefold.

Charts differ from graphs as to the *kind* of data which they present. Whereas line graphs, histograms, pie charts, and pictographs display data that were basically *statistical*, the flow chart presents data that are *descriptive* in nature. The chart describes *integral components and functions*. It usually illustrates how each part functions with respect to the whole system.

Organizational charts are similar to flow charts in that they present the overall structural plan of a group or an organization. Such charts usually indicate "chain-of-command" or hierarchical relationships of one part of the organization to the other.

Below is a chart which combines the features of both a flow chart and an organizational chart. It indicates a marketing organization structure arranged on three status levels: the top, the middle, and the operative. At the top of the organization is the president of the firm. Directly below the president are four departments: marketing, production, finance, and industrial relations. As a function of the marketing department are four other subdepartments: advertising and promotion, sales, marketing research and marketing services. Immediately answerable to the sales department are the operative force of four salespersons—or, perhaps more realistically, the entire sales force, here represented by a token group of four individuals. This is the *organizational* structure. The flow structure is indicated by the heavy black line in which the president holds the marketing department responsible for reaching a goal of $2 billion. The responsibility for this goal flows directly to the sales division, and from the sales division to each member of the sales force.

The central point to remember with all graphical material is that the author is attempting to convey a broad, overall idea or, as in the case of the chart below, ideas. The one idea is that of total organizational structure; the other the flow of responsibility for sales goal achievement. These two messages are presented simultaneously with one chart.

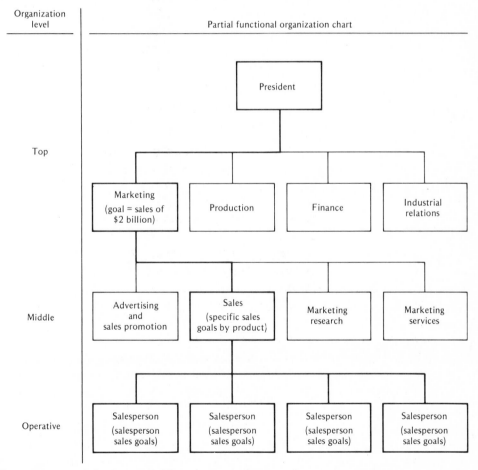

From Encyclopedia of Professional Management, edited by Lester Robert Bittel. New York: McGraw-Hill Book Company, 1978, page 794. Reprinted by permission.

The same main idea behind the graph may be presented variously according to presentation. The graphical *form* may differ, the idea remains the same. Above, the goal for sales achievement of $2 billion was expressed in one way, and we read the chart from top to bottom—although there is no good reason why it may not be read with equal comprehension in reverse. In fact, Hellriegel and Slocum present such a chart which must be so read in presenting the idea of an end-means chain and hierarchy of goals for part of an electric utility. Here is that chart. Five goals are expressed, each dependent upon a preceding goal which is the means by which the desired end may be achieved.

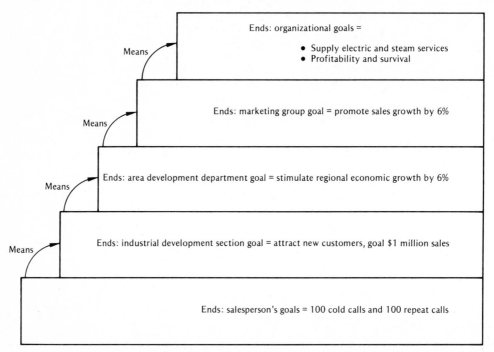

HIERARCHY OF GOALS AND THEIR DEPENDENCIES (From Encyclopedia of Professional Management, page 795. Reprinted by permission.)

Informational charts are somewhat different from the organizational type which we have just been considering. Informational charts aim to present in graphic form certain items of information, certain factual presentations in a form that will result in the greatest visual impact upon the reader. In thus doing, the author must sacrifice the precision of accuracy for the impact of the message. Note the graph below; it presents the health spectrum, with the central goal that of psychosocial and bodily health—the total well-being of the individual. Graphs, such as the one following, need considerable study to appreciate their *total* message. Considerable *information* is presented by means of one chart.

Notice that the chart suggests that the central goal of total well-being is dependent upon and surrounded by an all encompassing area of five factors: population, cultural systems, mental health, ecological balance, and natural resources. The arrows in this outer orbit also suggest that these five factors are also mutually interactionary: one affects and conditions the other, each acting upon its two adjacent neighboring factors—the one to the right and the other to the left of it. These five factors also result in four input-to-health influences, each differing from the other in relative importance—and this variation of magnitude represented by the width of the individual arrow. According to the chart, environment (comprised

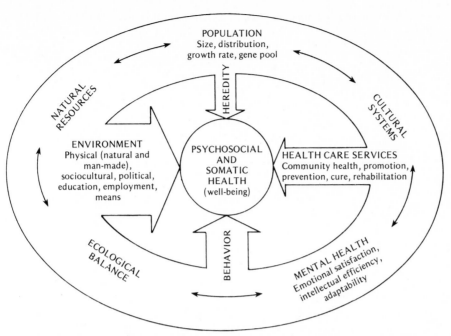

THE HEALTH SPECTRUM. (From Rockwell Scholtz and Alton Johnson, Management of Hospitals. New York: McGraw-Hill Book Company, 1976, page 5. Reprinted by permission.)

of its various elements) would seem to suggest that this is the most important factor in the individual's total well-being. Behavior comes next. Third in importance in the total well-being of the individual are the health care services, and finally, genetic determinants and heredity are of least importance.

Doubtless, we might be able to derive many more meanings from the chart—the origin of the arrows, for instance, the implications for conservation and the relationship of human well-being to national and international issues. The chart is pregnant with meaning. It suggests a great reservoir of factual information lying below its surface from which a myriad of questions may arise; and in the resolution of which, research, commanding the endeavors of an army of researchers, may take generations or even centuries to resolve. Such are the implications of a single chart. Such is the function of research.

TABLES

A table is a systematic presentation of data, usually *nominal* or *numerical* in character, and arranged in grid fashion. The numerical values are presented in parallel columns, each of which bears an appropriate heading describing the *type* of data or the organizational category to which it belongs. In the graph, these designations are comparable to the designations along the horizontal axis. Corresponding to the values on the vertical axis of the graph are the *specific* categories to which the columnar data refers.

Above, we presented two pie graphs.[9] To see the raw data used in constructing those graphs, we present the following table:

---

[9] See page 52.

TABLE 1. CONTINENTS, INCLUDING ADJACENT ISLANDS

Continent	Area			Population		Density of Population	
	(1000 mi^2)	(1000 km^2)	(%)	(thousands)	(%)	(per mi^2)	(per km^2)
Africa	11,709	30,319	20.2	352,764	9.8	30	12
Antarctica	5,396	13,975	9.3	0	0	0	0
Asia	17,069	44,211	29.5	2,075,726	57.8	122	47
Europe	3,954	10,239	6.8	636,529	17.7	161	62
North America	9,416	24,386	16.3	314,748	8.8	33	13
Oceania	3,452	8,942	6.0	21,166	0.6	6.1	2.4
South America	6,884	17,834	11.9	189,252	5.3	27	11
World	57,880	149,906	100	3,590,185	100	62	24

How to read a table. Tables are such common features in research reports that everyone who would read research and understand it should acquire the skill of reading tables. Essentially all tables follow the same format. We shall use the table which we have presented above as an example in discussing the various parts of a table and how to read them.

First, read the caption of the table. It indicates the general topic covered by the table. Here it deals with "continents, including [their] adjacent islands." Under the caption and usually between parallel lines are the *headings* for the various columns of data. Frequently, as in the example, the major headings will have subheadings. Under the heading, "Area," are three subheads: 1000 mi^2, 1000 km^2, and %. Translated these mean: "Multiply each of the figures below by 1000 to find the area in square miles (mi.^{2})," and, correspondingly, multiply each of the figures in the second column by 1000 to find the area in square kilometers. The "%" column indicates the percentage of the land area of each continent to the total land area of the earth. The two columns dealing with population are read in like manner. Add three zeros to the figure given under the heading "thousands" to get the correct population figure (e.g., Africa has a population of 352,764,[000]). The percentages are, again, the percent of the world's population which that particular continent contains. The area and the population percentages are represented on the respective pie graphs. Finally, the last two columns indicate the density of population "per mi^2" and "per km^2"—per square mile and per square kilometer. These columns are read in numbers of persons per square mile and per square kilometer. The figures at the bottom of each column present the total for that particular column.

Second, inspect each column for gross aberrations in the data. Look for extremes. Read *down* each column. Then, read *across* the columns, left to right. Have a note pad. Jot down any gross deviations in the data. Where are the extremes? Which item is largest? Which smallest? Do you discern any ratios between the individual items? As you inspect the column of figures, what is apparent? What items raise questions? Which ones are noteworthy? All these questions should be running through your mind. They should also have concerned the researcher. You should find evidence in the report that the *researcher* was curious and investigative with respect to these and similar matters. The researcher should see the meaning behind the data. He should *analyze* them and *interpret* them in the report. That is the researcher's responsibility, but the reader of research should also be aware of it.

Research reports which merely offer uninterpreted tables of data or uninterpreted graphs fail to fulfill the most basic requirement for research. To expect the consumer of the research to seek meaning from the raw data is to expect too much. As a reader of research, you should know this; and when a table or a graph appears in a research report, it should never be an end in itself. The reader of research has every reason to expect that those data that are thus presented will be directly related to the problem and have a role in its solution, and that the researcher will have established this connection clearly.

For example, as we inspect the table on the sizes and population densities of the various continents, depending upon the problem under investigation, some very apparent facts may—or may not—be relevant. They do, however, lurk within the columns of that table. And *that*, for our concern here, is all that is important. Stop reading at this point; go back to page 58. Look at the table intently and inquiringly. What do you see in the data there displayed that is noteworthy.

Perhaps we should pause at this point to discuss the nature of data and ways to interpret them. Data are like a jewel. Turn a jewel and you see it as a potential source of a myriad rainbow hues. As the jewel is turned, it reveals to the observer what otherwise cannot be seen. So data. As the researcher inspects them, they reveal different *meanings*. To the researcher, data have but one purpose: to provide a channel through which unsuspected meaning may be discovered. And this suggests a third way of looking at a table.

Rearrange the data within the table; try the data in different combinations. We note that under the three divisions in the table we have been examining—area, population, and density of population—we have indeed some gross aberrations of the data: extremes which are at once apparent. Asia, for example, is an abnormally large land mass and has a monumental population. It has the second greatest density of population of any continent on earth. By contrast, Antarctica is one of the three smallest continents and has no population.

These are immediately obvious facts. Now let us consider those data by rearranging them in the table. We shall *rank* the continents according to the three general divisions of the table. We shall rank them first in *area*—from the largest to the smallest; next, in *population*—from the most populous to the least so; and, finally, with respect to their *density* of population. We may be surprised what a slight change in position, like the turning of a gem, will reveal in the data.

RANKING OF THE CONTINENTS
FROM THE GREATEST TO THE LEAST MAGNITUDE
IN AREA, POPULATION, AND DENSITY

Area	Population	Density
Asia	Asia	Europe
Africa	Europe	Asia
North America	Africa	North America
South America	North America	Africa
Antarctica	South America	South America
Europe	Oceania	Oceania
Oceania	Antarctica	Antarctica

In the table on page 58, the order was alphabetical, from *Africa* to *South America*. That is a convenient and conventional method of listing, but it has no rationale *so far as the data are concerned*. What has the sequential arrangement of continental masses according to the initial letter of their names to do with the data relating to their characteristics? And the answer is: Absolutely nothing. What has the ranking of the continents according to some characteristic inherent in and expressed by the data to do with the rationale for their sequential arrangement? Perhaps it may prove very important. This brings us to a subpoint under the general heading we are discussing. That subpoint, and guideline, is this: *Look carefully at the left-hand column of any table; notice the determinant for its arrangement; consider how this method of determining the order of listing relates to the data which the table presents.*

By its very nature, a table is a somewhat rigid form for the presentation of data. It can have only one arrangement. But, even so, the researcher should then analyze the table pointing out its "hidden" meanings to the reader of the research—or at least as many of these "hidden" meanings as are appropriate to the solution of the research problem.

We have certainly not exhausted the interpretations that can be drawn from the facts in this table. Here are a few of these that you should have discovered when you went back, as we suggested that you do on pages 58-59, to reexamine the table:

1. *The area of Asia plus the area of Africa is just about equal to the combined areas of all the rest of the continents.*
2. *The population of Asia plus the population of Africa comprises just about two-thirds of all the people in the world.*
3. *Three-quarters of all the people in the world live on one land mass: the supercontinent which is comprised of Europe and Asia.*
4. *The area of Africa plus the area of Antarctica equals the area of Asia.*
5. *Africa and North America have just about the same density of population, with three more people per square mile living in North America.*
6. *Europe is the most densely populated of all of the continents; Oceania (except Antarctica), the least.*
7. *All of the people in North and South America equal only 25% of the population of Asia.*
8. *The area of North and South America combined is just slightly less than that of Asia, and about four times that of Europe.*
9. *South America is about 75% the size of North America.*
10. *Africa has only 55% of the population of Europe but is three times as large.*

These ten facts—and perhaps many more—are lying wrapped up in the data presented by the table. *Extracting meanings from the data which a researcher has at his command is what is meant by interpretation of the data.* We have just interpreted some of the data in the table. Perhaps it is important that we understand precisely the meaning of the word *interpret*. The word has several meanings, but they all point to the process of discovery and dissemination: to explain, to translate, to expound the meaning of, to render openly and clearly what is otherwise puzzling and hidden.

We have been discussing only one type of table: the *statistical* array in tabular form. Like charts, however, tables are of several kinds. As we had the informational chart,[10] so we have the informational table. This is an array in which information is presented in columnar form. It is a summary device for presenting essential information with respect to any given category. The categories are usually arrayed sequentially and vertically in the left-hand column. Then, horizontally, other columns present relevant information according to their several headings. Take the regulatory agencies and commissions of the United States Government. Here is an informational tabular presentation of the name of the commission, the year of its formation, the number of members composing it, and the purpose of the regulatory body.

REGULATORY AGENCIES AND COMMISSIONS OF THE UNITED STATES GOVERNMENT

Name of Commission	Year of Formation	Number of Members	Purpose
TRANSPORTATION			
Interstate Commerce Commission	1887	11	To regulate interstate surface transportation, to approve routes, grant certification, and ensure that rates and services are fair and reasonable.
Civil Aeronautics Board	1938	5	To promote and regulate civil air transportation, and to approve rates, routes, and agreements involving air carriers.
Federal Maritime Commission	1961	5	To regulate waterborne foreign and domestic offshore shipping of the United States and to ensure financial responsibility for indemnification of passengers and for cleanups of oil spills.
UTILITIES			
Federal Communications Commission	1934	7	To regulate interstate and foreign communications by radio, television, wire, and cable. The commission grants operating authority and approves interstate communication rates.
Federal Power Commission	1920	5	To regulate interstate aspects of electric power and natural gas to ensure reasonable rates and adequate supply.
CONSUMER PROTECTION AND COMPETITION REGULATION			
Federal Trade Commission	1914	5	To promote fair competition in interstate commerce, to prevent false advertising and deceptive practices, and to ensure true credit cost disclosure.
Consumer Product Safety Commission	1972	5	To protect the public against unreasonable risks of injury from consumer products, to establish product safety standards, and to ban hazardous products.
EMPLOYMENT			
Equal Employment Opportunity Commission	1964	5	To investigate charges of employment discrimination and to bring actions before the appropriate Federal District Court.
National Labor Relations Board	1935	5	To investigate and settle labor disputes and to prevent unfair labor practices.
Occupational Safety and Health Review Administration	1970	3	To adjudicate cases from the Department of Labor respecting safety and health inspections.

[10] See page 56.

Name of Commission	Year of Formation	Number of Members	Purpose
ENVIRONMENT AND TECHNOLOGY			
Environmental Protection Agency	1970	Administrator	To abate and control pollution through standard setting and monitoring.
Energy Research and Development Administration	1974	Administrator	To consolidate federal activities relating to research and development on the various sources of energy, to achieve self-sufficiency in energy.
Federal Energy Administration	1974	Administrator	To ensure a sufficient supply of energy to the United States, to evaluate allocation, to plan storage and rationing.
National Aeronautics and Space Administration	1958	Administrator	To conduct research on space flight and exploration.
FINANCE AND INTERNATIONAL COMMERCE			
Commodity Futures Trading Commission	1974	5	To strengthen the regulation of trading in futures and all commodities traded on commodity exchanges, to protect market users from fraud and other abuses.
Export-Import Bank	1934	President of the bank	To grant loans and issue guarantees and insurance so that exportation may be undertaken without undue risk.
Federal Deposit Insurance Corporation	1933	Chairman	To promote confidence in banks and to provide insurance coverage for bank deposits.
Securities and Exchange Commission	1934	5	To protect investors and the financial community against wrongful practices in the securities markets. The SEC relies on disclosure requirements to, as well as regulation of, securities dealers.
U.S. International Trade Commission (formerly U.S. Tariff Commission)	1916	6	To provide studies and recommendations concerning international trade and tariffs to the President, Congress, and other government agencies; to conduct investigations especially with respect to import relief for domestic industry and antidumping.

Sometimes in tabular form, and belonging half way between a chart and a table, we meet another type of graphical presentation of information such as the table below. The table presents research findings based upon investigations done at the National Bureau of Standards in Washington, D.C. Each intersection of the following chart contained an original research problem. Go back to page 2 to review the definition of a research problem. Take the first intersection in the table. The question that needed resolution was: In hand-washing cotton materials, what is the recommended type of fabric care—warm water or cold? And the *facts* indicated that both were equally recommended. Not so with linen materials. The facts indicated that hand washing with warm water only was superior in caring for this type of fabric. So the information is presented throughout the table. Here is what the researchers at the National Bureau of Standards found.

The table has resulted from a series of experiments designed for one purpose: to resolve "those tantalizing, enigmatical, unresolved roadblocks to knowledge [in the caring for various fabrics] for which no answer had as yet been [definitively] found." That is research. The table presents the conclusions of the researchers by means of a black dot in the proper space.

RECOMMENDED TYPES OF FABRIC CARE

Method		Cotton	Linen	Silk	Wool	Acetate	Tri-acetate	Acrylic	Anidex	Glass	Metallic	Moda-crylic	Nylon	Olefin	Polyester	Rayon	Rubber	Saran	Spandex	Vinyon
Hand Wash	Warm	•	•	•	•	•	•	•		•	•	•	•		•	•			•	•
	Cold	•		•	•										•			•		
Machine Wash	Hot	•																		
	Warm	•	•				•	•	•	•		•	•	•	•		•	•	•	•
Tumble Dry	Hot/Normal	•	•												•					
	Warm/Delicate	•	•					•	•	•		•	•	•	•	•			•	
Drip Dry	Flat Surface				•						•				•					
	Line Dry	•		•		•				•					•	•	•	•	•	•
Dry Clean		•	•	•	•	•		•		•	•				•	•	•		•	
Do Not Use a Strong Detergent				•	•						•				•	•	•	•		
Do Not Bleach			•	•	•	•					•				•	•		•		
Iron	Low Heat Set			•	•	•			•	•	•									
	Medium Set	•						•	•				•		•	•				
	High Set	•	•				•													
No Ironing Required										•					•	•	•	•	•	•

Source: National Bureau of Standards

Speaking of the way in which research relates to a table, the table on page 64, indicating some aspects of the product life cycle, may illustrate this relationship clearly. We have two aspects of the product life cycle: (1) the profit levels expected, and (2) the competitive market structure. In the product life cycle there are four stages: (1) introduction, (2) growth, (3) maturity, (4) decline. The interaction of the one aspect on the other at each of the four stages creates problems at that stage which may be appropriate for research investigation. These problems are listed in the section designated as "typical problem mixes." Study the following table. Note the research opportunities it suggests.

As we have remarked earlier, interpretation of the data is a primary responsibility of the researcher. Simply to foist upon the reader uninterpreted graphs and tables is nothing more than irresponsible fact-collection and fact-disposal—it is not research. Also, to give the reader a graph or a table or any other mass of data without its being carefully and closely related to the problem is unfair and unreasonable. The reader of research should not be burdened with the task of interpreting raw data, but consumers of research should know what the interpretation of data involves, so that a more intelligent decision can be made as to whether the researcher is fulfilling *his* role and responsibilities adequately.

The language of line and column is a form of communication that needs much more attention, that says much in little space, and that requires interpretation before its meaning comes through loud and clear. The suggestions of this chapter may assist in making that language less cryptic and more expressive.

SOME ASPECTS OF THE PRODUCT LIFE CYCLE

Aspects \ Stages	Introduction	Growth	Maturity	Decline
Profit levels expected	Losses can be expected due to heavy costs of research and development, etc.	Increasing profits due to higher sales and decreasing unit costs for promotion and production.	Profits peak early in this stage and then start to decline due to more firms joining the "bandwagon," which results in intense competition, price cutting, etc.	Rapid decline in profits due to decreased sales, cut-throat competition, decreasing economics of scale.
Competitive market structure	Little competition unless rival firms are introducing similar products. Promotional efforts by competitors are likely to promote product rather than brands. Since consumer preferences are not stabilized, market share fluctuates.	Competition is still limited, especially for products requiring greater technological know-how. However, if the technological barriers are low, promotional efforts play an important role in determining the market share that will ultimately result.	Competition becomes much more intense, and market share stabilizes due to the development of preferences based on earlier purchases. Because of a larger number of products with similar characteristics, price plays an important part in determining market share.	Because firms have sunk costs and market sales are declining, competitors are willing to cut prices almost to the level of marginal costs. Generally, only strongly entrenched firms can hold on to their market share.
Typical problem mixes—information needs for pertinent decisions	1. Consumer resistance to adoption due to reluctance to change existing behavioral patterns, etc. 2. Uncertainty regarding the extent and nature of the market. 3. What product features are important to make it a success? How to emphasize them? 4. Distribution problems due to item 2.	1. Estimation of the impact of competitors' strategies. 2. Should profit levels or market share be maximized? 3. Who are the customers? How should they be cultivated? 4. Are any product improvements necessary? 5. Is the distribution system adequate?	1. How can we induce customers to use the product more frequently? 2. What are the characteristics of "heavy" users? 3. Can the product be modified or improved to stimulate sales? 4. Are there ways to increase the efficiency of the distribution system? Can profits of intermediaries be restricted without endangering market share? 5. Can we stress any attributes of our product to make inroads into competitors' market share?	1. How rapid is the decline expected to be? 2. Should the firm withdraw from the market? 3. Is it worth the expense to try to reawaken interest? 4. What are the advantages of new competing products? Can these be offset?

From *Encyclopedia of Professional Management,* page 697. Reprinted by permission.

_ _

Practical Application of the Preceding Discussion

    Project 1. On pages 37-38, we discussed the dynamics which are at work upon any phenomenon that is depicted upon the crossed lines of the grid. For this

Phenomenon Depicted upon the Grid	Dynamic Exerted upon the Data from the Ordinate	Dynamic Exerted upon the Data from the Abscissa
1. The germination of a bean	*Growth force, measured in inches of growth*	*Time force, measured in elapsed days.*
2.		
3.		
4.		

project, locate ten graphs. Using the form of a table, such as the one skeletonized on p. 64, account for the forces interacting upon the data. As an example, we shall fill in the first item from the instance of the growth of the bean. (See graph p. 36.)

Project 2. On page 37, four general types of graph line configuration are outlined. In the ten graphs you have collected (in photocopy) identify the type of activity which each graph line portrays. The discussion on pages 37 to 42 may assist you.

Project 3. Find five histograms. On graph paper, replot the data in the form of a line graph. According to the type of data being presented, which do you consider to be the better representation of the character of those data? What do you notice in the line graph that is not so obvious in the histogram, or vice versa? Be able to defend your opinions.

Project 4. Photocopy each type of graph discussed in this chapter. Beneath each, discuss the graph comprehensively in the light of the material presented in this chapter. Evaluate the appropriateness of the graph to convey the message inherent in the data.

Project 5. Below is a graphical representation of a family's race with inflation over six salary increase periods. Assume that the salary increments came at equidistant intervals. The graph to the left shows income; the graph to the right expenditures. Explain the lines. For example: in the left-hand graph, the cost of living line climbs steadily. In the right-hand graph, the item of taxes is shown as increasing from $2,680 to $8,240; while the cost of groceries shows a declining line from $2,540 to $4,920— and yet, the graph is correct. Explain. As a pair, the

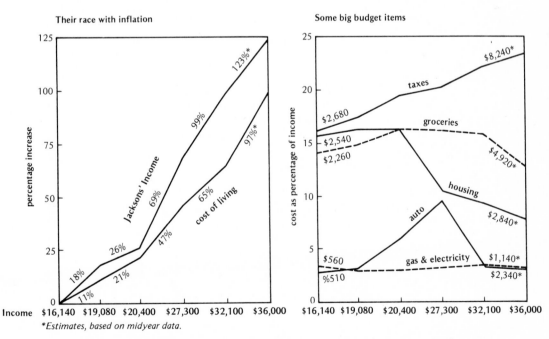

From Changing Times: The Kiplinger Magazine, Vol 33 (October, 1979), p. 10. Reprinted by permission.

graphs are very interesting. Point out any other features which you find note-worthy.

Project 6. The purpose of this project is to give you some practice in reading tables and in applying the guidelines and directives given in the chapter from pages 58–63.

On page 31 is a table presenting the raw data for the research study reprinted from the *Journal of Counseling Psychology,* "On the Tendency of Volunteer Helpers to Give Advice." Analyze that table. List all of the discoveries that you can find, seriatim, as was done on page 60. Study the table thoroughly.

_ _

CHAPTER 5 It's a Fact!

What's a Fact?
What Kind of Fact?
Beware of Fact-Pollution!
Fighting Fact Contamination
The Truth, The Whole Truth, and Nothing But . . .

Facts are the researcher's stock-in-trade. They are as essential to the researcher as bricks are to a mason or lumber to a carpenter. Without facts, the researcher is out of business. Yet researchers seldom call facts *facts*. They call them *data*. *Data* is the plural form of the Latin word *datum*, which in turn is the noun derived from the verb *dare*, meaning *to give*. Hence, data are those facts or principles given or presented to a researcher from the environment around him. Sometimes data are defined as "pertinent facts" and if pertinent, then they must be pertinent to something, and that "something" is merely the problem which the researcher has under investigation.

WHAT IS A FACT?

"It's a fact, I tell you; it's a fact!"
Words similar to those we hear frequently in everyday conversation. We speak of facts as though they were commonplaces—which, of course, they are, if we think no further than a tacit everyday assumption. It's like saying, "This is a book that you are reading"—which, of course it is, if we think no further than a superficial statement about it. But when we think of a book in terms of the skill of editor, designer, and printer who put it together, we get a little more insight into what "this is a book that you are reading" means. Think further. Behind editor, designer, and printer is the mind of the author and all of the thinking and organizational processes that brought the words of the book together. Let a nuclear physicist think of a book and, in the ultimate reaches of his thought, he will see in the paper an in-

tricate organization of fibrovascular tissues comprised of atoms, each with its complex and characteristic nuclear structure; in the ink on the page, a complex molecular system comprised of the molecules of carbon, kerosine, and the other ingredients of printer's ink. The statement, "This is a book that you are reading" is a simple statement with multifaceted implications. So with a fact.

Because facts are so all-important to research, because an architect, a contractor, a builder need to know intimately the composition and quality of the materials that go into a structure, so you as a consumer of research should have some insight into the basic raw material of the research process.

What *is* a fact? Let's look at some characteristics of facts, which, of course, researchers call the *data*.

Facts are abstractions. In common parlance, we speak of "finding the facts." And yet, if someone asked you to go out tomorrow morning and not to come back until you found a fact and brought it back with you—you would never return! Facts are elusive insubstantial figments of our thought. No one has ever *seen* a fact. We discussed in the last chapter the fact of growth, and we saw what the *effects* of growth were—in the bean, in the Spanish population. Researchers—and all of us, for that matter—speak of "presenting the facts," but seldom do we recognize that what we utter is more metaphor than reality.

Facts are the way we identify our trustworthy observations. All the data that a researcher gathers are largely the result of observations of one kind or another. Long chapters ago, when we discussed the scientific method, we summed up the whole methodology of that quest for truth in a few words: "Look, see, record; look again, see a second time, record once more. Believe what your eyes tell you, what your senses proclaim."[1]

In our indomitable quest for truth, we have a boundary beyond which we may not pass: the boundary of our five senses. In the great world around us, all that we know of it, the totality of which we can be aware, must come to us through the channels of five input routes. Only when we can convert electromagnetic radiation to sound from a loudspeaker, so that we may *hear* it, or to waveforms upon the face of a cathode tube, so that we may *see* it, do we know *for a fact* that it is there. Whether signals from outer space, beyond the range of visual sight or camera's peering eye, or whether from deep within our own bodies, by the ultra-delicate techniques of biofeedback, all that reaches us must claim the attention of our awareness only after it has been converted into *sensory* data.

Thus, like comprehending the concept of a book, we see that the more deeply we probe into the nature of a fact, the more mystical and elusive it becomes. It may have been that the monks of the Middle Ages realized this, and so sought truth by the way of revelation and mystical insight. The line between mystical intuition and absolute Truth is very tenuous indeed.

What we call facts is merely a way of identifying observations of the phenomena around us. But the paragraph subhead added one more word, *trustworthy* observations. Merely to observe is not enough. We must observe with the provision that we can trust what we see, what we hear, what we otherwise sense. Ice must *always* be cold, solid, and melt to water. A crystal of common table salt must *always* be cubical, composed of equal parts of sodium and chlorine, and have a characteristic saline taste. The sense data that we receive must be worthy of our trust and *verifiable* repeatedly: the same circumstances should always produce the same results. If so, we might accept what we have observed as a *fact*.

---

[1] Page 10.

Some facts are elusive and ephemeral. When scientists at the nuclear reactor laboratory at the University of California confirmed the theory of P.A.M. Dirac as to the existence of antimatter, the fact that confirmed the theory lasted only for a billionth of a second and produced only a faint meteor-like tracing on a photographic plate. That, of course, is an extreme case. But, as readers of research, we must be eternally vigilant as to the generalizations that a researcher draws from data of the antimatter type. Caesar's *Gallic Wars* begins: "I came, I saw, I conquered." Much of the data in the battle for the discovery of new knowledge or the resolution of old problems might be: "It is, it was, it's gone—forever!"

Much research utilizes ephemeral data; and, as consumers of research, we should recognize that fact and make due allowance for the conclusions that ensue as a consequence.

We are interested in studying the drinking habits of adolescent youth.[2] We wish to know more about the influence of peers and parents on teenage drinking. We select a senior class of 331 boys and 323 girls in one of the public high schools in Albuquerque, New Mexico, and we give each student a questionnaire inquiring about his or her drinking habits. What comes back to us from the answers on the questionnaires are *facts—data*, as we should properly call them. We process and analyze these data and we are prepared to draw certain conclusions, which the authors of this study have done, with respect to drinking among seniors in high school.

But wait! We have overshot the mark. As discerning readers of research, we note that *that is not what was found at all*. What we discovered was what 654 boys and girls in a specific senior class, in a specific high school, in a specific city, in the State of New Mexico *told us* about their drinking habits *at a particular time*.

Can we extrapolate these findings and generalize from this about the drinking habits of all seniors in American high schools? No. Can we consider the findings applicable to all New Mexico youth? No. Can we conclude that all Albuquerque city high school seniors fit this drinking pattern? No. All that we can conclude is that *it would appear* that we have learned something about the drinking habits of 654 senior class students in *one high school* of all of the Albuquerque high schools, and that this may be a very fleeting discovery at best.

Consider how ephemeral these findings really are. Within a few months, this class will graduate and the individuals will disperse, so that never again will this group exist—as high school teenagers. The stream of life moves on. Each individual will change. Some will stop drinking entirely, others will have different attitudes about it. A class of 654 boys and girls will have vanished forever and in its place 654 individuals, each with changing ideas, living under new influences—college, employment, married life—will have no single cohesive force to bind them together.

The facts that were gathered in this study were *elusive:* we could not be sure that these students were telling the absolute truth in responding to the questionnaire; and they were *ephemeral*, because as those students sat there, answering those questionnaires, some of them at that moment may have been altering their thinking about drinking. The class is gone now—forever. Their thoughts, their attitudes, their individualism-of-the-moment have all vanished. The facts that we secured, the data that we studied, were snatched from a fleeting moment that will never come back again.

This sobers us indeed in making generalizations with respect to any research. For conclusions are no more valid than the facts that support them, and so as readers of research,

[2] Morris A. Forslund and Thomas J. Gustafson, "Influence of Peers and Parents and Sex Differences in Drinking by High-School Students." *Quarterly Journal of Studies on Alcohol*, Vol. 31, No. 4 (December, 1970), pp. 868–875.

we need to inspect that body of fact very carefully, seeing it for exactly what it is—a meteor-like trace across the complex fabric of life.

What was found may have been "the truth" for a fleeting moment only: while the students actually marked each questionnaire response. To go beyond that with any kind of certainty is to venture into an investigative quicksand.

Facts vary in quality. Not all facts are the same. Some reflect the truth with much greater fidelity than others. Facts that have the highest level of truthful reflectance are those that are frequently called primary facts or *primary data.* Primary facts originate as close as possible to the absolute Truth, which they purport to express.

Originating further away from the source of absolute Truth are other facts which are commonly referred to as *secondary data.* All research seeks to rely only, if possible, on primary data. To do so is to risk less chance of error creeping in because of inaccuracy within the data themselves. Take an example. We are interested in describing the motion of the eyes as they sweep over a line of print in reading. Exactly what happens when one reads a line of print? The process was first described by a French professor at the University of Paris. It is the earliest description we have to date, and it was published by Professor Louis Emile Javal in 1879 in a French journal, *Annales d'oculistique,* under the title "Essai sur physiologie de la lecture." Now, a later writer purporting to translate Javal's words described eye movements as "little hops" across the line of print. If we are to accept this description we are relying upon another's rendering of what was actually written. What was written? How were eye movements first described? We must go back to the primary source—the "Essai" itself. Here are the words:

> . . . *l'oeil subit meme plusieurs saccades dans le courant de chaque ligne, ...*[3]

Did Professor Javal describe the movements as "hops"? No. The word he used was *saccades.* Now what is the difference between this word and "hops"? The words suggest diametrically opposite ideas. "Hop" means to leap forward. But that was not at all what Javal meant to convey. The word "saccade" perfectly describes the muscular involvement in the eye movement, for it means "a quick, violent check of a horse, by a single pull, or twitch, of the reins." That is exactly what the muscles of the eye do.

The words of Professor Javal are primary data. The purported translation, secondary data—and what a difference the one was from the other! Have you ever played the party game where all the players sit in a circle: the first player whispers a sentence to the second, who in turn whispers it to the third, and so on around the circle? And when the last person reports what he heard, it bears no resemblance to what was originally said. So data become distorted when they stray too far from the original source. The best research relies upon the words of the person who whispered the idea *first.* Hearsay, whether it be of the scholarly variety or neighborhood gossip, is never a preferred substitute for the first utterance.

So then, what is a fact? We have been considering all of its facets. We have described its characteristics. Now, let us try to define from a functional standpoint what a fact really is. *A fact is the most trustworthy observation of things and events in an individual's environment and experience.*

---

[3] Louis Emile Javal, "Essai sur physiologie de la lecture," *Annales d'oculistique,* LXXXII (Novembre–Decembre, 1879), p. 252.

CLASSIFICATION OF DATA

Since researchers must work with facts of all kinds, it is necessary that this universal body of fact assume some organization. We have, therefore, an organizational system for data, whose terminology you may meet in reading research and which you will certainly need to understand for an appreciation of some of the statistical manipulations of the data, which we will consider in the next chapter.

Facts are facts; but they must not become one monumental disorganized mass. We classify data in several ways.

According to the inherent quality of the data. Think of a stream; think of the rocks that lie in it. These two comparisons exemplify data. One type of data, one kind of fact is *discrete:* composed of separate and distinct parts, individually independent. And there are many facts, much data, that belong to such a category: rocks and sand, men and women, boys and girls, pears and peaches, chairs and tables—and we could go on *ad infinitum.* There are also those facts, like the stream, that are indivisible, continuous, attached, conjunctive. These data are called *continuous* data. Of such are streams, molasses, time, infinity, one's own age, the atmosphere. None of these come in little pieces. They are one continuous fact.

According to the way in which the data are measured. To all facts, we can apply some scale of measurement, some order of differentiating one fact from the other. Generally, we measure data in four ways: by *name,* by *order of sequence,* by *assigning them a value and measuring the difference between the value assigned to the one and the value assigned to the other,* and by *measuring how many times the one is larger or smaller than the other,* this is a *comparison* technique. These four ways of identifying data are called, for convenience: *nominal data, ordinal data, interval data,* and *ratio data.*

Nominal data. To measure the data nominally, we simply give each fact, each group of data, a name. It distinguishes these from all others. It also assigns them a designation which sets a limit to their individuality, and by so doing, thus "measures" them against other individuals or extraneous groups. For example: desk, tree, Margaret, Henry, and so on.

Ordinal data. Measurement sets limits and within those limits arranges the subparts in a specific order. Consider a foot rule. The limits of the foot rule are 0 at the one end and 12 at the other end. Thus, we take a series of inches and arrange them in the order of 1, 2, 3, 4, 5. . . to 12. We can also measure the months of the year by setting them in order from January to December. We measure the length of the alphabet by setting the letters in order A to Z.

Interval data. Interval data are those data which are measured in terms of the difference in standard units between one object and another. For example: 15 degrees east of due north measures the distance on a compass rose from 0, which is true north to 15, which is 15 degrees east of magnetic north.

Ratio data. When we measure data by the ratio scale, we compare one item with another in terms of multiples: ten times more powerful, twice as effective, four times as long. We usually think of the ratio scale as beginning with zero. If we think of a yardstick as being three times as long as a foot rule, we start from zero to establish the limit of the foot rule. Then, the *ratio* of three to one establishes the comparison *in terms of multiples* between the foot and the yard measure.

According to the number of groups from which the data originate. We can classify data in terms of the milieu out of which the data originate.

One-group data. These data arise out of a single group or a homogeneous setting; as in case of the data which result from a testing-teaching-testing situation. In such a procedure, we usually reason that if the second testing shows an improvement over the first testing, then that improvement has resulted because of the teaching. This, of course, may or may not be so, and we shall discuss the matter later in this chapter.

Two-group data. On page 20, we discussed the experimental method. There, we discussed the way in which two groups are selected. One is kept uncontaminated by any treatment which is given the second group. At the outset both groups are evaluated or tested. At the conclusion of the experiment, a second evaluation or testing takes place. A comparison of these two evaluations may reveal that the group which was kept uncontaminated from the treatment which the other group received will show little change while the "treated" group may show a significant change. If so, we attribute the change to be the result of the "treatment" of the second group.

Many-groups data. Sometimes research designs can become somewhat complex. For example, we are conducting an experiment in which the data are derived from studying an inner-city population. The members of this population come from a sub-section of the city in which there are well-defined national communities: the Russian, the Irish, the black, the Hispanic. Data arising from such a conglomerate situation must be treated differently from that arising from a homogeneously-selected two-group situation.

According to the number of variables the data contain. In reading research studies, you may be constantly confronted by two terms with respect to the data. One of these describes the data as a *constant,* the other as a *variable.* These two terms we should understand thoroughly. A *constant* is a value or a concept which is always the same under identical circumstances. Under the pressure of one atmosphere, for example, water always boils at 100° Celsius. The ratio of the circumference of a circle to its diameter is always 3.14159265+. Each minute always contains 60 seconds. A *variable* is a concept or a value which fluctuates—usually in relation to an extraneous factor. Watch a barometer. The atmospheric pressure that it records is a variable. For those interested in solar energy, the amount of sunlight from day to day—hour to hour, for that matter—is a variable.

While we are dealing with constants and variables, perhaps this is the place to introduce another term which you may encounter frequently in reading research. That word is *parameter.* What is a *parameter*? A *parameter* is a function, a characteristic, a quality of a population or other data-related situation in which the *concept* is a constant, but whose *value* is variable. A parameter, therefore, is a strange kind of half-breed quality which is, in fact, a commonplace reality. For example: consider these two squares:

Each square has a *surface area.* That area is a parameter of the square. The *concept* of area is always the same: it is the product of one side multiplied by itself (squared). No matter what size the square, that *concept* is always *the same.* But the *value* of the side is quite another matter. That *varies* with each square of differing size. Thus, the area of a square is *one* of its parameters; a side (of the square) is another.

We shall have more to say about parameters in the next chapter, when we consider the statistical implications of research. But, let's get back to the discussion of the classification of facts according to the number of variables they contain.

Univariate data. Univariate data relate to those facts which are constants except for one variable in the universe or population of fact. The familiar Snellen test for visual acuity is an excellent example of this type of data. The person being examined remains the same. The ambient light within the examining room remains the same. The distance to the target remains the same. Only the point size of the letters projected upon the target screen *vary*. All factors remain constant except the one being studied: the ability to read smaller and smaller type.

Bivariate data. As the term itself suggests, these are data in which there are *two variables*. We are studying the effect of ambient light upon the accuracy of a class in typing to reproduce a given selection. We have two obvious variables: the variation of illumination, which we regulate from brilliant to threshold-of-vision intensity, and the level of typing skill which will presumably differ with each student.

In reading research, you will meet two other varieties of variables: *independent* and *dependent variables*. These are terms we identify largely with experimental research methodology. An *independent variable* is one over which the researcher has complete control. He can manipulate it at will. In the example which we cited above with respect to illumination intensity and typing effectiveness, the illumination intensity is the independent variable. With a rheostat switch, the experimenter is able to control precisely the number of lumens that fell upon the copy from which the students type. The frequency of typing error or efficiency factor is the *dependent* variable.

Other authors designate these two variables differently. Van Dalen[4] calls attention to this fact and gives the broad range of terms applied in lieu of those used here.

The Independent Variable	*(causes)*	The Dependent Variable
Other names applied to this term by some investigators are:		*Other names applied to this term by some investigators are:*
cause		effect
stimulus		response
antecedent		consequent
experimental variable		behavior variable
treatment		effect

Multivariate data. These are data which contain within them three or more variables. With such data, each variable must be isolated and studied by a somewhat sophisticated tool, multivariate analysis.

---

[4] Deobold B. VanDalen, *Understanding Educational Research: An Introduction.* (New York: McGraw-Hill Book Company, 1962), p. 222.

To summarize all that we have discussed with relation to the classification of the data, the following organizational chart may bring all of the discussion together.

DIAGRAM SHOWING THE CLASSIFICATION OF DATA

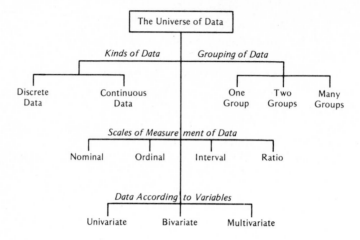

BEWARE OF FACT POLLUTION!

Any microbiologist will confirm the fact that we live in a microbe-polluted world. They are everywhere—those little microorganisms: in the air we breathe, the food we eat, the clothes we wear, on whatever we touch, inside of us, outside of us. It is impossible to live in a biologically sterile world.

We are not alone. Facts are also subject to infection. In its severe form, it can render the fact unfit for use by the researcher, just as infection in its severe form can render the human body useless in performing its normal routine.

Fact-contamination is called *bias*. Bias is any influence which results in the data being distorted, or any deviancy—no matter how minute—whether caused consciously or unconsciously, which results in the fact's inability to report the truth absolutely.

Bias attacks the integrity of the fact. It renders data suspect. It casts a shadow of doubt over the whole research situation when it becomes so pronounced as to be clearly recognized. And researchers must be continually vigilant in planning research so that as little bias as possible will enter the research design.

A small Midwestern city is planning the erection of a multi-million-dollar library, to be paid for out of the municipal tax funds. The community is devoted to civic improvement; its citizens are broad-minded and educated. I go out to survey the man-on-the-street to find out exactly what the average citizen thinks about the feasibility of such a project. My results show that 20 percent of those surveyed are in favor of the construction, 70 percent oppose it, and 10 percent have no opinion. I am stunned by what I have found out. But there are the facts—the honest responses of honest people.

But are they? The town is a university city. I make my survey during the month of August when practically the entire university community is away on vacation. My results, therefore, are not the opinions of those who would almost certainly favor any improvement which would result in the betterment of the intellectual life of the community. Nor, have I seen the headlines in the morning's paper that ABC Corporation expects to move to a city in the South. That means a big loss of tax dollars to the city treasury. The month is August, when most of those who are on the street are the middle to lower income bracket workers upon whom an additional tax burden for a new library may fall most severely.

Have I sampled the opinion of the community? Not really. Probably had I chosen a bright day in mid-October when the *Morning Journal* carried no depressing headlines, the results may have been entirely different, and the ratios may have been reversed. What I experienced, however, was a pronounced bias. Had I sampled the community in October, I may have had more responses from the university segment; I may have had some response from those who were away on vacation in August but were available for opinion polling in October. The psychological shock to the community may have been softened and prospects may not have looked nearly so bleak to so many of the population as they did on that day when the moving of the ABC Corporation was announced. All these factors influenced the data adversely on that August morning. The facts were contaminated with bias. This, however, is an extreme example, and a hypothetical one. Bias need not be so blatant on the face of the fact.

Many times bias is subtle and surreptitious—but nevertheless quite as destructive to a true reading of conditions within the universe of fact. In interviews, a glance, an emphasis or stress in speaking—no matter how slight—the whole personality of the interviewer may be just enough to elicit coyness, or caution, or ultra-frankness on the part of the interviewee, thus introducing distortion, be it ever so small. In questionnaires, the wording of certain questions or the burden of their subject matter may cause the recipient of the questionnaire to withdraw and to answer the question calculatingly and with much cautious calculation. For example, in these days of widespread drug addiction, can you imagine what caution a question like the following might elicit from many respondents:

Have you ever used (even with a doctor's prescription) any of the following drugs:

	Yes	No
Amphetamines	——	——
Barbiturates	——	——
Cocaine	——	——
Diazepam	——	——
Marijuana	——	——

And yet, for a study of how individuals begin the dependence on drugs, such a question may be perfectly reasonable and necessary. We need not have much imagination to realize, for example, what a question to parents as to whether their children ever had any encounter with the police might bring in responses.

In their reports, some researchers print the instruments they have employed in soliciting the data. As a reader of research, it may be well for you to study these documents carefully in an attempt to assess the role that the instrument may have had in introducing bias into the report.

Bias is not a cause for apology or avoidance on the part of the researcher. It is a fact for recognition. As none of us need to apologize for the fact that we are microbe-ridden, so researchers need not be sensitive about the probable presence of bias in their studies. Honest acknowledgment that bias may be an uncontrollable factor may, in fact, do much to enhance the honesty of the researcher and the integrity of the report. Legally, bias is an openly recognized fact. In jury selection, prospective jurors are always asked as to whether they have any preconceived ideas about the innocence or guilt of the accused, whether they have any interest in the case which would preclude them from judging the case fairly and without prejudice, and so forth.

Bias may creep into the design of the research itself. How was the population for the study chosen? A researcher reports that a telephone survey was made of 1,875 families in the community and that ... . But what does that fact tell you? It clearly indicates that this was a *selected* population, even though the names were chosen by sheer chance. Those whose names do not appear in the telephone book are those in the community:

1. Who have unlisted telephones, and consequently are perhaps the professional people of the community or well-known persons—in short, those presumably of the upper socioeconomic status who do not wish to be bothered by unwanted telephone calls.

2. The newcomers to the community whose names do not as yet appear in the directory.

3. Those who have no telephones because their income level is so low that they cannot afford a telephone.

Hence, a bias is built into this method of gathering data, because the data, regardless as to how randomly selected, is slanted toward the middle-income class and toward residents who have lived in the community at least a year or more.

Perhaps one of the classic examples of bias is the famous "Hawthorne effect." The designation Hawthorne comes from the location where the research was carried out: The Hawthorne Plant of the Western Electric Company. Workers in three departments of the company were inspecting small components: switches, relays, and coils. The hypothesis was that if the intensity of the illumination within the plant was increased, accuracy and efficiency in worker performance would be noted. Sure enough. The light intensity was increased, the worker efficiency showed marked improvement. One puzzling factor, however, was present. Even though the light was then decreased, the worker efficiency inched *ahead* slowly. Further experiments were carried out: intermittent rest periods, varying the length of the working day—the result, regardless of the manipulation of the design factors—was still the same. Worker efficiency continued to improve, slowly and irrevocably. Some factor was causing the improvement to take place. Some influence was creeping into the system. Some bias was present that was not being accounted for. Finally, it was concluded that it was the *added attention given to this group of selected employees* out of all of those working at the Hawthorne Plant that made the difference and accounted for the increase in production. The term *Hawthorne effect*, therefore, has come to mean any situation in which a subject, participating in an experiment, will tend to improve his performance merely because of the additional attention given him. Such attention helps the ego—the mere fact of having been chosen. It spurs motivation: the individual wants to prove himself worthy of the distinction that has been afforded him. These are slippery elusive factors, but they do tend to alter the individual's performance. Beauty queens tend to outcharm their ordinary charm. Those selected for the Olympic contests tend to increase their performance merely because of their selection. The force at work is bias.

FIGHTING FACT CONTAMINATION

Given the fact of bias—and there are literally thousands of ways in which data can be influenced by external and uncontrollable factors—what safeguards can be taken to minimize its effect? There are several of these, and we shall outline them briefly.

The right attitude on the part of the researcher. The human being is a fascinating creature. People see what they want to see. They hear what they want to hear. They find facts supporting the positions that they endorse and the issues they espouse. If, therefore, the researcher has strong prejudices, inflexible beliefs, bigoted opinions, the chances are that such a researcher may have a tendency to *interpret the facts* in line with his preconceived ideas. He will see in them what he wants to see. We say, "He will be *biased* in his thinking." Bias of this type is deeply rooted and almost humanly impossible to overcome. As a man thinketh, so is he—unfortunately! Books written to espouse a cause or evidence proffered to support a belief are scarcely research. They are little more than prejudice manifest and we should recognize the shortcomings of such biased attempts.

We mentioned earlier the caution that is exerted in choosing jurors. One matter that is usually thoroughly explored is the matter of prejudice. A prospective juror who is known to have openly expressed the attitude: "I hate purple people a day old!" will probably not be an impartial juror in a trial involving the guilt or innocence of a purple prisoner.

Researchers who have deep and abiding prejudices toward a problem in research would do well not to attempt to research it. Bias will probably ruin their effort.

This type of bias is especially devastating in historical research. If you are a loyal son or daughter of the South, and the last defender of the Confederacy, it may be well for you not to attempt to research the battle of Gettysburg. It is just possible that all the saints may have been arrayed along Seminary Ridge and Beelzebub and his demonic forces may have been across the Emmittsburg Road on Cemetery Ridge, and try as you may, you will never be able to see the battle in its true historical perspective with two fine generals confronting each other in life and death struggle.

A controlled situation vs. an experimental situation. Another way to try to control the effect of bias in the system is to set up as nearly as possible parallel situations. One of these is sealed off from any contact with the experimental process, the other situation is exposed to experimental influence. For example, we have two plants side by side. Both receive the same amount of sunlight, the same amount of rain; both are subject to the same variations of ambient temperature and air pollutants. One plant is given 10 cc. of a mixture consisting of four drops of ammonia and a drop of chelated iron in a quart of water twice a week for eight weeks. The other plant is given nothing but pure distilled water. The second plant is the control. The plant receiving the ammonia-iron treatment is the experimental plant. After eight weeks, each plant is evaluated for growth, general health, and other factors. There can, of course, be no bias here. No? We did not say that the ammonia-iron solution was to be made of pure distilled water. Unless it was, there is a slight possibility that the trace minerals in the water used in the solution may have made the difference. Bias is extremely ubiquitous.

Sometimes we set up experiments involving human beings on the control-experimental design format. We take one group of students and we "match" them with another group of students. One group we call the control group: the other group, the experimental group. Then we do something to the second group that we do not do to the first group. We measure the difference between the groups. We conclude that what we did to the second group made the difference. In making such a conclusion, we forget, however, that we can never be sure that we have two "matched" groups. Two people never equal each other. Each is a unit—an individual, different from any other individual. If you, then, have 20 individuals in each group which you have carefully "matched" as to sex, race, and I.Q., it does not mean that you have assembled 20 stereotypes. Seen properly, you have the most intricate, complex, interacting set of dynamics possible within each group. It is only by the farthest stretch of the imagination that we can think of them as having any similarity. And yet, we have thousands of experimental studies each year based upon just such a design: control group–experimental group design.

It is, of course, the best we can do. Twenty sixth-grade boys and girls with I.Q.'s that range between 100 and 110 are taught geography by two different types of maps. One group uses the conventional flat textbook type of map—an approach that is standard for all students in the school system. The experimental group is taught by three-dimensional relief maps. During the study, they never see a flat map. Then after 16 weeks of such teaching, we compare these groups in terms of their comprehension of the geographical features of the earth. We probably see a difference. We attribute the difference to the type of map that was used in teaching the class. We cannot forget the influence of bias, however. Each teacher is different. Each class is different. The surroundings for each group are different. The presentation of subject matter and the discussion of topics may vary from one class to the other. The factors of home environment are different for each individual pupil. We ought not let our naïveté deceive us. And, with such a broad and complex spectrum of factors that may introduce biases by the score, as readers of research we ought to look very carefully at what safeguards were introduced to minimize the effect of bias in such experiments.

Careful researchers usually provide for some criteria for the admissibility of the data. Not every fact that comes to our attention is suitable for research purposes. Facts must be screened. They must be made to meet the standards that will attempt to insure the greatest degree of reliability of the data and the least detraction from their credibility because of the presence of bias.

The placebo approach. When drugs are tested for their efficacy in producing the effects they are supposed to produce, pharmacologists usually divide the population upon whom these drugs are tested into essentially a control and experimental dichotomy. All patients are given capsules that look precisely alike. Some of these capsules contain the substance under investigation. Some capsules contain flour or sugar or some other such innocuous substance. The patient does not know whether he is getting the drug being tested or whether he is merely getting the *placebo.* The researcher knows, of course. This is one way of overcoming any bias of psychological origin.

Randomization. This is another method of selecting members of a research group to insure that the presence of bias or other external influence would not affect the data. Randomization is usually employed in selecting samples from a larger population so that the selection is made as much as possible by pure chance. This obviates any possibility of a selection which favors any predetermination of choice. Randomization can be effected in a number of ways. Basic to all random sampling, however, is the fact that as nearly as possible absolute fortuitousness—pure chance—must govern the selection of the sample. The purpose of this is so that the sample will be as much like the total population from which it was chosen as is possible. We shall see the reason for this in the next chapter when we discuss inferential statistics. The accuracy of making a prediction with respect to the total population from the minipopulation depends upon valid randomization. Any dissimilarity between the total population and the sample increases the predictive error. And, even with chance selection, we cannot be sure that the sample will reflect accurately the characteristics of the total population. Even a series of samples drawn from the same population and carefully compared with each other will show some slight differences among them; and this, also, we shall discuss later when we consider the *error of the mean.*

How, then, is randomization accomplished? There are several methods.

The lottery method. Selecting a random sample by the lottery method consists of giving each person in the population a number. If there be 100 persons in the total population, then each person is assigned a digit from 1 to 100. One hundred slips are also numbered and placed in a container. Then without seeing the slip that is being drawn, an assistant draws a slip from the previously mixed and tumbled slips. It bears a number. That number is recorded and the person to whom that number is assigned in the general population becomes the first chosen to comprise the sample. Then the slip is thrown back into the total number of slips. In this way we always maintain in the reservoir of slips a pool of 100 from which to draw. This also gives a 1:100 chance of being selected. If the same number is drawn that was previously selected, it is tossed back and a new drawing is made. The process goes on until sufficient individuals have been selected to form the sample to be studied. Obviously this is a method for relatively small populations.

The roulette wheel method. Another method is appropriate for small populations where a number can be placed on a roulette wheel and this number corresponds to a numbered individual in the population. The wheel is spun. When a number comes up, it is listed and the person whose number corresponds to the one that appears on the wheel is selected as a member of the sample group.

The table-of-random-numbers method. Here selection is made by employing a so-called Table of Random Numbers. Tables of this sort consist of blocks of numbers randomly selected and provide a means of random selection. Part of a table of random numbers may appear as follows. We present merely a sample.

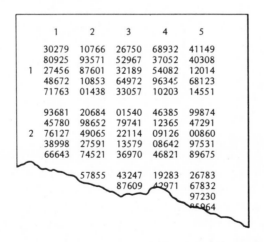

	1	2	3	4	5
	30279	10766	26750	68932	41149
	80925	93571	52967	37052	40308
1	27456	87601	32189	54082	12014
	48672	10853	64972	96345	68123
	71763	01438	33057	10203	14551
	93681	20684	01540	46385	99874
	45780	98652	79741	12365	47291
2	76127	49065	22114	09126	00860
	38998	27591	13579	08642	97531
	66643	74521	36970	46821	89675
		57855	43247	19283	26783
		87609	42971	67832	
				97230	
				85964	

PARTIAL TABLE OF RANDOM NUMBERS

The way of using a table of random numbers is to let chance decide who will be chosen. Let us say we will have 75 in the population. The table must be "entered." Entrance into the table must be fortuitously and by mere chance. We must find two digits. We close our eyes and open a book at random. We will take the left-hand page number and, if this be a three-digit number, we will choose the last two digits. Upon opening our eyes we see that the number of the left-hand page is 111. The last two digits are "11." This means that we will start with row 1, column 1. We shall take the last two digits in each random number from top to bottom. Looking back at our table, we find that these digits are 79 (which we cannot use because we have only 75 in the population), but 25, 56, 72, 63 which we can use. Going straight down column 1, we come to 81 and 80 (which likewise we cannot use because they are more than the population); then to 27, which is acceptable; 98, which is unacceptable; and 43. Previously we have had the members of the entire population select a number from a random pool of numbers. We are selecting a sample of 35 out of the 75. The first 35 digits that we can use from the table will give us our sample.

The telephone book method. Lacking a table of random numbers, we might open a telephone book at random, and taking the last two digits of the listed numbers, if we have a population less than 100, or the last three digits, if we have a population from 100 to 999, and use these digits in the same manner as we did with the table of random numbers.

Out! Bias, out! All we have been attempting to do with these various methods is to circumvent the entrance of bias. We are trying to protect ourselves from any possible accusation that the data which we used were contaminated. If pure chance dictates decisions, then we cannot be suspect on any counts of using biased data. We have protected the purity of the fact insofar as possible.

Careful researchers will take occasion to indicate how they have attempted to counter the probability of bias—particularly in those situations where bias may be readily recognized as a likely element to be guarded against.

Facts are facts, but like the delicate petals of a flower that can be stirred by the slightest breeze, facts are also prone to contamination, as we have previously discussed. Let us be alert in reading a research report to recognize whether bias may have had a more than normal probability of entering the system and, if so, whether the researcher made every effort to protect the fact—to guarantee the integrity of the data—and indicated that precaution to the reader of the research. It is only reasonable that this should be done.

THE TRUTH, THE WHOLE TRUTH, AND NOTHING BUT . . .

This chapter opened with words to the effect that without facts there would be no research. The remainder of the chapter was devoted to examining the nature of a fact, the characteristics of a fact, and the contaminating influences that may warp and twist facts so that they are unfit for a true exploration of the problem for which they are secured. Ultimately it is the fact, and the manner in which the fact has been acquired, the safeguards that have been observed to preserve the integrity of the fact, and the defenses that have been erected to shield it from those influences that would bias it and becloud its purity, that are important not only to the researcher but also—and perhaps *more* so—to those who read the report that the researcher has issued, *because* the facts lie at the very heart of the research process: the *why* and the *how* upon which the *what* depends.

As a reader of research, you should examine the report for some indication of the care that the researcher took with the facts. You have every right to know *how* the facts were secured, what the population was from which the facts were gathered, what *method* of random sampling was employed in assembling the sample, what *criteria* the researcher established for the admissibility of the data into the study, what *means* were used in the interpretation of the data, *in summary form* what the data were that were used to support the conclusions and resolve the problem, what the *conclusions* were that were dictated by the data—all of these matters are a part of the structural framework which supports the research effort and gives validity to the research report.

A recent news release reports that much research is shabby and unprofessional—especially when it is designed to lure government money for a sponsored research project. In their haste to secure grant funds, some researchers short-change the whole proposed endeavor. The concerns that we have raised in the paragraph above, grant applications are loath to spell out or consider at all. This means that we should read a research report very carefully, with minds buzzing with the questions that we have proposed from time to time with respect to the methodology and, in fact, the entire research project.

One further matter: they who deal with facts should have an orderly mind, a practical and realistic approach, and be able to express the thoughts presented in the report in clear, coherent, and comprehensible prose. The old wive's tale that researchers can do satisfactory research but cannot write a readable and communicative report is broadly accepted. Report writing does not demand literary skill. It simply requires an orderly mind that can think to the point, keep thoughts together that belong together, to be able to read one's one words to decide whether they communicate accurately what the researcher intends to say, or—in fact—what the words on the page *do* communicate—if anything.

Let's take an example. Several years ago a study was made of "The Relationship of Job Satisfaction to Perceived Staff Promotional Policies."[5] Here is the statement of "methodology" with relation to that study. In the paragraph preceding the one which we quote the "perceived staff promotional policies were defined as having four dimensions" and then the "four dimensions" were listed. The discussion of methodology followed.

Methodology

Indices were devised to measure each of these dimensions[1] and combined into a questionnaire[2] administered to public high school teachers.[3] Two-hundred and fifty responses—twenty-five from each of ten schools—were randomly selected[4] to be used in the analysis. The responses were scored so that a low score on the job satisfaction scale would indicate a teacher had a tendency toward low job satisfaction. A low score on the perceived staff promotional policies scale indicated that a teacher had a tendency toward believing that staff promotional policies discourage local staff members from entering administration.

Now, let's look at that paragraph. We shall attempt to read this brief section of the research report and to understand it. The exponents in parentheses were inserted in the paragraph at points where the careful reader of research might pause and question the report. For example:

---

[5] Robert N. Kirkpatrick and the California Teachers Association from *California Journal of Educational Research* 15:76-81, March, 1964. Reprinted in Edwin Wandt, *A Cross-Section of Educational Research* (New York: David McKay Company, Inc., 1965), p. 145.

1. "Indices *were devised* to *measure* each of these dimensions." *How* were these indices devised? What was the rationale behind the devising?

   They were devised *to measure*. Measure *how?* Measure by *what scale*, by *what standard?* Just to tell us that they were devised to measure the dimensions is to ask the reader to take on faith a great deal that is essential to the study. What we need here are *facts*: specific indications as to how the indices "were devised" and of what the measurement consisted. Earlier in this chapter we indicated four ways of measuring data.[6] To which of these scales did the "measurement" of the data belong?

2. ". . . and combined into a questionnaire . . ." *What* was combined into the questionnaire? The indices? If I can read correctly, that is precisely what the report says: "Indices were devised . . . and combined . . ." I confess that I am somewhat puzzled at this point how "indices" can be "combined into a questionnaire," but that's what the report says, and so it must be. And it furthermore says that this questionnaire, comprised of combined "indices," was administered "to public high school teachers."

3. Public high school teachers? *What* public high school teachers? and *where* were they teaching? In a particular school system? In a particular area? Anywhere in the United States? The report fails to indicate the population, except for this foggy identification! You'd get a lot different response from the high school teachers of the Watts area of Los Angeles than you would from those in Santa Barbara or Monterey. What we need are *facts* to appraise the possibility of bias.

4. Now, we are told that 250 responses—25 from each of 10 schools were "randomly selected." By what method of randomization? The great specter of Bias comes over the horizon again at this point. How are we to know *how* that selection was made, and how "random" it really was? Being stuck with a questionnaire composed of indices, I am somewhat skeptical at this point on the matter of randomicity. I do not question that it was "random"; I simply want to know as a critical reader of research *how that randomicity was achieved—* and any reader of research who will be asked later to accept the "conclusions" of the study has a right to know this, and researchers should feel obligated to provide it. What I need are facts, *facts, facts!* Without specific indications not only as to *what* was done, but *how* it was done (and this would have taken only a few words additionally), I am unable to evaluate the statement. I have a feeling that I am being exposed more to what the researcher did autocratically than what the *facts* would have indicated was best to be done.

5. "The analysis"? *What analysis? What* was analyzed and for *what* purpose? This is the first allusion to an *analysis.* I note that 250 responses were selected to be used *in* the analysis. Were any other data also used *in* the analysis, or were the 250 responses the only data that were *analyzed?* If so, why not say so? Then I would have no doubt that the 250 responses comprised the *total data* subjected to analysis. The wording is confusing.

---

[6] See page 71.

In this brief section of the report, I find more generalization than specificity; more telling *what* was done, rather than an explanation of *how* and *why* the researcher did it. It is these last two items that are important to the reader of research. To have merely the end product—the *what*—without any means of judging the rationale of the research process—the *why*—and of the methodology to accomplish it—the *how*—is to provide the reader with very little upon which to appraise the research as a whole.

We have perhaps commented sufficiently on this brief paragraph. The purpose of this brief critique has perhaps served its purpose, which was, of course, to apply the suggestions of the foregoing chapter to the reading and understanding of an actual research report. The chapter has discussed facts, the presentation of facts, the need for facts in the presentation of a research effort. The report should be factually compact.

— —

Practical Application of the Preceding Discussion

Project 1. Make a list of 25 facts. Classify these facts according to the several categories indicated from 71 to 74. You might make a form such as the following presenting your information in tabular array using the following suggested format:

Fact	Classification of Fact			
	Kind of Fact	Grouping of Fact	Measurement Scale	Variables

Project 2. Read five research reports. Study the conclusions of each report carefully. Classify the data as to the degree of their ephemerality. Are the conclusions generalized beyond the ephemerality of the data? e.g., does the writer of the report imply that these conclusions are permanently valid without recognizing the fact that they are circumscribed by time and, perhaps place, of occurrence?

Project 3. Survey studies and experimental design research are particularly susceptible to bias. The words, "a random sample was selected . . ." tell you very little. Likewise, the statement that "a sample was selected by randomization" may be but the repetition of a research shibboleth. It tells you essentially nothing. Also, in experimental studies, statements such as "group 1 was considered to be the control group while group 2 was the experimental group—without any further elaboration—is nearly meaningless. Survey some studies to see if you notice any such generalized statements of methodology without any specific indication as to what these statements really mean. What facts does the writer of the report offer to buttress the generality by citing a specific methodology approach?

Project 6. The purpose of this book is to help you to develop discerning and critical skills in reading and understanding research. Here is a research study. You are asked to read it and to react to it critically; and critical, in this sense, does not mean "fault-findingly." It means discerning the excellencies as well as those items which, in your opinion, need more data to assist you in making a fair and impartial judgment. We have printed the study on half-page format so that you might react with your own comments opposite the section of the text where you deem comment is necessary. Show, by your comments, that you have comprehended all of the material in this text to this point. *This critique is not limited to the material in Chapter 5. It should reveal your understanding of the entire book and show that you know some ways in which to read research and understand it. You may wish to annotate your comments by placing in parentheses, following each one, the page or pages of the text where you find the discussion relating to the subject of your comment.*

School Children's Problems as Related to Parental Factors

Jack Rouman

The following article deals with a real community and the problems of its children. In experimental studies such as this, the large global problems are left behind for specific examination of special issues.

It is commonly held that working mothers contribute to disturbance in children. Teachers often say, "Well, it's no wonder he is in such bad shape. His mother works." Causes are easy to ascribe if one does not test the assumptions. Here is a typical assumption put to an experimental test. Also demonstrated in this article are some of the methodological difficulties involved in trying to ascertain the factors behind the development of certain behavior patterns. You may see here something akin to Langdon and Stout's work in the preceding chapter.

This Column for Your Comments on the Study

Today we find much emphasis placed on the mental health of school children. Those engaged in working with these youngsters are well aware of their emotional difficulties, but there is still more we need to learn as to the causative factors.

Considerable research has been done with respect to the relationship between the psychological climate of the classroom and the child's emotional health. But today we are confronted with certain contemporary problems that call for serious consideration. Among these are the unusual number of mothers employed outside the home, and also divorces—creating step-parents and guardians, and involving frequently the absence of an adult male in the home.

These latter factors have received a great deal of public attention and have often created considerable anxiety on the part of the parents involved. It has become necessary, therefore, to determine the degree and manner in which these contemporary elements affect the school child.

From **Understanding the Child** (a quarterly journal published by the Nat. Assn. for Mental Health, 10, Columbus Circle, New York 19, N.Y.), Apr. 1955, 24:50–55. Reprinted by permission of author and publisher.

The findings and conclusions in the present report are derived from case studies of children in the Montebello Unified School District of Los Angeles County, California. This school district, with approximately sixteen thousand pupils, includes kindergarten through twelfth grade, and contains socio-economic areas that make it fairly representative of most communities. Reference is made to approximately four hundred active case studies serious enough to be carried over for a follow-up by the district's guidance department staff during the 1954–55 school year. Case studies centered upon physical handicaps and mental retardation are eliminated from the present report.

We also include here statistics on children of Mexican parents. Since this is a cultural problem that districts like ours are seriously concerned with and try to handle adequately, we need to learn all we can about the special problems of the group. They constitute 12 per cent of the total number of the district's case studies.

The four hundred cases we have will be divided into four categories: (1) Where the mother is employed full time away from home; (2) where the children are living with step-parents or guardian; (3) homes in which the adult male is absent; (4) homes which do not have any of the above factors present (to serve as a control group).

STATISTICAL DATA

In 18 per cent of the cases the mother was employed full time away from the home (15 per cent in the Mexican group); 16 per cent of the pupils live with step-parents or guardians—25 per cent of these having mothers employed full time. Homes in which the adult male was missing were represented by 12 per cent of the cases; 50 per cent of these had mothers employed full time (7 per cent of the Mexican group). The control group was limited to 18 per cent of the remainder of the four hundred case studies (selected at random) in order to make a comparative picture. It should prove significant that altogether we find approximately 25 per cent of the total case studies represented by employed mothers.

GROUP I (employed mother)

	Per cent
Academic failure	28
Aggressive behavior	28
Withdrawing behavior	33
Nervous tendencies	8
Stealing, sex, etc.	3

GROUP II (step-parents and guardians)

Academic failure 40
Aggressive behavior 30
Withdrawing behavior 10
Nervous tendencies 15
Stealing, sex, etc. 5

GROUP III (lack of adult male)

Academic failure 50
Aggressive behavior 20
Withdrawing behavior 15
Nervous tendencies 10
Stealing, sex, etc. 5

GROUP IV (control group)

Academic failure 40
Aggressive behavior 30
Withdrawing behavior 20
Nervous tendencies 8
Stealing, sex, etc. 2

REASON FOR REFERRAL

We shall look first at the major reason given by the teacher in referring the child for guidance services.

From these data "academic failure" and "aggressive behavior" appear as the two major problems. The percentages differ significantly, however, among the four groups.

It will be noticed that, apart from Group III, problems involving aggressive behavior represent approximately one-third of the referrals. Academic failure is greatest among pupils lacking an adult male in the home. Another factor found in this study will shortly be presented, which seems to help us understand better the reason for this situation. The child with a working mother displays the greatest percentage of "withdrawing behavior." Before attempting to draw conclusions as to specific reasons for these findings, however, we need to study other possible factors.

AGE AND SEX OF THE CHILD

There is need to know what ages and sex are more susceptible to certain parental factors. The following statistics provide a picture of this phase of the problem. The ages are grouped by grade level, so several analyses can be made with a single presentation. The girls constituted approximately 25 per cent of the case studies.

These data indicate that the youngest children in Group I are most affected by the employment of their mothers and that the older children are able to make a better adjustment to the situation. This should be a most significant fact for parents to keep in mind if the mother's employment is not a matter of dire necessity. It was found, however, that the older girls resented the domestic responsibilities placed upon them when the mother was working away from the home.

The reverse appears to be the case in Group II—children living with step-parents and guardians. Here the younger children are able to make the better adjustment, while the older child finds the new relationship difficult to accept. Likewise the step-parent finds it difficult to understand the child—thus aggravating the problem. There were only a couple of cases at the ages of fifteen and sixteen. Further investigation disclosed that many of the older youngsters had not only begun to leave school but to leave their homes as well. The older girls, however have the biggest problem here, since they are not able to be emancipated as readily as the boys from the home environment.

GROUP I (employed mother)

Grade	Age
Kdg.—Primary	5–8
50% (10% girls)	
Elementary	9–12
30% (5% girls)	
Jr.—Sr. High	13–16
20% (10% girls)	

GROUP II (step-parents and guardians)

Grade	Age
Kdg.—Primary	5–8
25% (5% girls)	
Elementary	9–12
50% (10% girls)	
Jr.—Sr. High	13–16
25% (15% girls)	

GROUP III (lack of adult male)

Grade	Age
Kdg.—Primary...	5–8
30% (5% girls)	
Elementary	9–12
50% (5% girls)	
Jr.—Sr. High	13–16
20% (10% girls)	

GROUP IV (control group)

Grade	Age
Kdg.—Primary...	5–8
45% (10% girls)	
Elementary	9–12
40% (5% girls)	
Jr.—Sr. High	13–16
15% (5% girls)	

In Group III the elementary-age child, again, seems more affected by the lack of an adult male. It should be noted that the girls are of the smallest percentage in this particular group, in comparison with the other two parental groups. This leads to the conclusion that the female child is less affected than the male child by the missing adult male's presence in the home. However, the older girls represent the biggest percentage of girls in Group III. The reasons were found to be two-fold: (1) heavy burden of domestic responsibility; (2) lack of supervision.

The control group shows that the concentration of school children's problems is at the younger ages. We note an interesting fact, namely, that there are as many girls with school problems among the four years 5 to 8 as there are in the eight years 9 to 16.

ORDER OF BIRTH

Much is being said about the relationship between the child's order of birth and personality. Our study provided certain information on this point. We found, for example, that the youngest child in the family of the employed mother is more affected than any other. It is this child, apparently, who becomes the one most in need of attention if the mother seeks employment. Where there are step-parents or guardians, it appears to be the oldest-born child who is affected by remarriage and placement with guardians. It does not appear to be as serious a problem past the age of twelve.

Where there is lack of an adult male the only-born child appears definitely affected. We also know that the age span 9 to 12 is a most sensitive time for a child in this parental group.

One of the most striking points that came out of this part of the study is the finding that the oldest child in the family is most affected among the control group. We found that the age group 5 to 8 represented 45 percent of the control group referred for guidance services. This would imply that nearly half of the children in need of psychological assistance (other than those in the three types of parental groups involved in this study), although they are the oldest-born children in their families, are no more than eight years of age. We found some of the causative factors for this to be: (1) Birth having occurred at the time the parents were beginning to adjust to post-war conditions; (2) children competing within the same family, especially when the oldest-born child is young and still very dependent upon parental guidance; and (3) older-age children (and oldest in order of birth) finding enough opportunities outside of the home, to gain emotional security.

PERSONALITY COMPONENTS

Next we shall look at the personality profiles of the four groups to discover, still further, in what ways particular school problems are related to parental factors. The scores given herewith represent the percentage of the group falling below 50 percentile on the California Test of Personality. Since space does not permit a complete presentation of the scores, only those significantly higher or lower, in comparison with the other groups, will be shown.

Taking Group I first, we found these children to be lacking, to a greater extent than any other group, in feeling independent of others. They also feel a lack of cordial relationship with people in general. They substitute the joys of a phantasy world for actual success in real life. We previously learned that they represented the greatest percentage, in reasons for referral, under "withdrawing behavior." They lack a sense of security and self-respect in connection with their families. This feeling is carried over to school relations in terms of how well they feel liked by the teacher, how they enjoyed other pupils, and how well school work is adapted to their level of interest and maturity.

GROUP I (employed mother)

	Per cent
Self reliance	50
Feeling of belonging	62

Comments on the Study

Freedom from withdrawing tendencies 68
Family relations 56
School relations 60

GROUP II (step-parents and guardians)

Sense of personal freedom 54
Feeling of belonging 61
Nervous symptoms 70
Social skills 58
Community relations 58

GROUP III (lack of adult male)

Self reliance 39
Sense of personal worth 67
Sense of personal freedom 29
Family relations 35
Social standards 49

GROUP IV (control group)

Sense of personal worth 61
Feeling of belonging 64
Social skills 60
Anti-social tendencies 61
Family relations 54
School relations 59

Group II is made up of problems involving a sense of personal freedom, in that the child lacks a reasonable share in the determination of his conduct and in setting policies that will govern his life. This group equally suffers from a lack of cordial relationship with people, as was found to be the case with Group I. Although nervous symptoms were evidenced in every group, children living with step-parents and guardians seem to be under the greatest emotional strain. Another characteristic of children in this group is a lack of social skills. This helps us to understand why they are more often referred for aggressive behavior than children in the other two parental groups under study. The problem of community relations is explained by the fact that acquiring step-parents, and particularly guardians, often means moving away from friends and surroundings offering security and pleasure—a factor frequently overlooked.

Children in Group III, missing the companionship of an adult male, indicated that their greatest problem was in "sense of personal worth." The child lacks belief that he is well regarded by others and that they have faith in his future success. We recall that this group was most often referred for academic failure. Their case studies revealed that they were not lacking in capacity to any greater extent than the other groups, but did lack the motivation and standards often given and set by an adequate adult male in their growing stages. However, they were comparatively strong in self-reliance and family relations (in contrast with the group with employed mothers). These children have to learn to depend more upon themselves because of their particular parental situation, and usually have stronger loyalty and appreciation for the single parent trying to be both a father and a mother to them. A problem hardly existed, for this group, in "sense of personal freedom" (in contrast to the step-parent and guardian group). There was little family opposition to allowing these children to be emancipated at an early age from their home environment. But in social standards a problem did exist. Although the percentage found was not large enough to be alarming, it did indicate an area of serious weakness. Children lacking the adult male are also lacking in much of the guidance needed to understand what is regarded as socially right or wrong in one's society.

We discover that members of the control group form a composite of personality difficulties found in the other three groups. They are similar in the feeling of personal worth found in Group III; the feeling of belonging, of both groups I and II; the social standards of Groups II; and the family and school relations of Group I. However, they lead the other groups in antisocial tendencies. This helps us to understand why the child in this group is so often referred for aggressive behavior. The anti-social child attempts to get his satisfactions in ways that may hurt or be unfair to others.

Comments on the Study

CONCLUSIONS

A number of conclusions have already been cited, but there are several more that are important, and we need also to review some very significant ones.

1. We have found that the three parental groups involved in this study constituted approximately one-half of the children referred for school guidance services (excluding problems based upon mental and physical handicaps).

2. A working mother contributed to only one-fourth of the total number of cases in need of psychological help. Apparently there are many children whose mothers work, who do not present problems in school. This would indicate that as long as the child

is made to feel secure and happy the mother's full-time employment away from home does not become a serious problem. But if employment is sought, we must be most sensitive to the needs of the younger children.

3. The statistics disclose that the problem of the working mother is not as great among Mexican children as with the non-Mexican group; but their difficulty lies in the area of a broken home. Also, far fewer Mexican mothers attempt to raise their children alone.

4. We found that girls make up only one-fourth of the total number of cases referred for guidance services. Encouragingly, the overall difference between the total percentage found in the control group and those of the three parental groups is very little. It is at the later years that the girl is more affected by irregular change in her home environment.

5. The age and sex findings for the group lacking an adult male correlate well with data on growth development. The younger child, still more dependent on his mother, is not as handicapped as the elementary-age child, who needs his father's relationship to guide him in developing the necessary male characteristics.

6. It is important enough to repeat that children need a great deal of help in adjusting to step-parents and guardians. Their ability or inability to get along with other children is indicative of how well the adults in their home environment get along with them.

7. There is a definite relationship between the only-born child and our three parental groups. In comparison with the small number in the control group, we may conclude that the irregular home environment is a strong contributing factor to the only-born child's school problems.

8. Lastly, there may always be circumstances that parents cannot prevent to cause a child to be placed in one of these three parental groups. Nevertheless, these problems are of a controlling nature. A sincerely concerned parent or teacher, made aware of what might happen to a child under these particular circumstances, is in a position to prevent, or at least minimize, the child's difficulties.

— —

If Facts, Why Figures?
What It's All About
Where Is the Center of It?
How Broad Is the Spread?
Facts, Too, Have Relationships
How Much Is Due to Chance?

IF FACTS, WHY FIGURES?

We have just finished reading a chapter on facts and their importance in the research process. At this point, you may ask: If we have the facts, what else do we need? Are not the facts enough? The answer is: Not so!

Facts alone are like so many pilings for a pier. There they stand—singly, as units in themselves, grouped together but meaningless. They are like so many factual "sticks" emerging from a research problem area. They make no sense until they are coordinated. As a pier needs a superstructure to give meaning to the piling, so facts need to be considered collectively—not as separate and individual units, but as a total aggregation.

This "support mechanism," this means of coordinating, is provided by statistical treatment of the data. Facts by themselves are meaningless. It is only when they come together into constellations of related units that they become significant to the researcher. Only then do they reveal the meaning that lies below their surface.

This is the fundamental purpose of the scientific method.[1] It is accomplished by *inductive reasoning.* Consider the process of inductive reasoning as illustrated by the following schematic:

---

[1] See pp. 9–12.

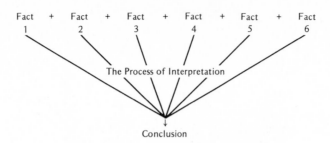

THE PROCESS OF INDUCTIVE REASONING

We have observed six facts. They are isolated instances, but as an aggregate they form a body of factual knowledge from which we can arrive at a conclusion. Each fact, in its own way, leads toward that conclusion, but it cannot be contributory to the conclusion until it has passed through the process which researchers call *the interpretation of the data.*

The word *interpretation* is of uncertain origin, but it has always been used in connection with *meaning.* Interpreters of old were those who revealed the meaning of occult happenings or strange events: Pharaoh of Egypt, who told of his dreams and found that there was none in his court who could interpret them until one, Joseph, was brought before him. Then the meaning of his dreams became clear. Interpreters turn the unfamiliar words of one language into comprehensible thoughts of another. Like words of a foreign language, facts also need *interpretation*, if their *meaning* is to be revealed.

Take history. History is a record of facts that have happened to the human race. But we need to make a distinction between a chronicler and a historian. A chronicler merely records the facts of current events. The historian, on the other hand, takes those same facts but, by asking the question, "What do these happenings *mean*?" turns a mere compilation of chronicled fact into the interpretation of history. To see the difference, read *The Anglo-Saxon Chronicle*, then read Arnold Toynbee, *A Study of History*. The difference between fact *recording* and fact *interpretation* will be evident immediately. The historian adds meaning to fact; the chronicler does not.

Interpretation needs a medium of expression to convey meaning. In research, that medium of expression is frequently *statistics. Statistics is a language* because, through it, the researcher is able to express what cannot be otherwise communicated. Most of the data of research come to us in numerical values: how much, how many, how long, how wide, to what degree. These concepts must be expressed in *numbers* instead of words. We must use another channel of communication if such ideas are to be expressed at all and if they are to be *meaningful* to any one. That channel is *statistics.* And, if you are to read research and understand it, you must have some general knowledge of what the researcher is attempting to say when the facts are presented in statistical language.

Let us go back to the diagram above. Instead of "fact 1, 2, 3, ..." and so forth, we shall present specific facts: the grades of a student on six successive tests:

$$73 + 88 + 79 + 92 + 88 + 96$$

What have we said? What do these grades *mean*? To most of us, as they stand, they do not mean very much. And whatever meaning we do derive from them comes to us expressed, not through the verbal channel of communication, but through the statistical one.

Now let's take these grades again and discover their meaning through the use of statistics.

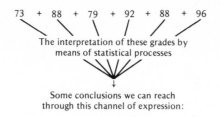

The interpretation of these grades by
means of statistical processes

Some conclusions we can reach
through this channel of expression:

STATISTICS GIVE MEANING TO GRADES

1. Student's average for the six grades is 86.
2. The grades range from 73 to 96: a range of 23 points.
3. The exact middle of this range of grades would be a grade of 88.

Not one of the foregoing three facts could possibly have been known without the assistance of statistics. Facts, alone, therefore, are not sufficient for the purposes of research. If facts are expressed numerically, and then these numerical values processed according to certain statistical operations, we may be able to gain added insight into the underlying hidden meaning of those data. Thus, statistics is in a very real sense a *language* which can communicate meanings which can not be comprehended in any other way.

There is nothing difficult about statistics and statistical procedures; but, if you are to read research and understand it, then you must be able to orient yourself to a statistical environment and feel comfortable when you are suddenly confronted with statistical concepts.

STATISTICS: WHAT IT'S ALL ABOUT

Most of us are frightened by the term *statistics*. It sounds ominous, complicated, over-our-heads. It's none of these. All of us have perhaps used statistical processes every since we have been able to add, subtract, multiply, and divide: for that's about all there is to statistics. But in research statistics are very important. Statistics can tell us something about facts which we cannot comprehend in any other way. And this is very important. But what *can* statistics tell us? Why do we use statistical procedures? How is the territory of statistics divided?

We need answers to these questions if we are to understand the function and role of statistics in the research process. We should be able to look down on the whole landscape of statistics, to see its major divisions, to understand its organization, to see one part in relationship to another.

On the next page is an organizational chart. It shows the landscape of statistics and the nature of its various areas.

Note that statistics is divided into two general categories: *parametric statistics* and *nonparametric statistics*. First, we need to understand the terms. *Parametric statistics* is that branch of statistics which is concerned with *parameters*. A *parameter* is a characteristic, a feature of a population that is represented by a *statistical concept*. Most parameters are merely *imaginary statistical constructs*. They are real in the sense that we speak of them as though they exist, when in reality they are merely figments of our statistical imagination. What are some parameters? The mean, the deviation, the coefficient of correlation—these are common parameters. They are concepts that are characteristics of populations. For ex-

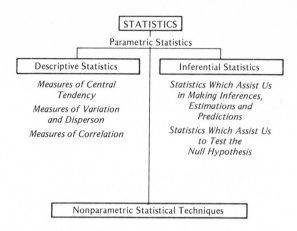

ORGANIZATIONAL CHART OF STATISTICS

ample, a *mean* or an *average* is a parameter. The dispersion of the data or the *deviation from the mean* is a parameter. *Degrees of relationship* are parameters. Perhaps, if we should define a parameter, and then see how this definition applies to the parameters we have just mentioned, we may be able better to understand just what we mean by a parameter.

A *parameter* is a characteristic of a population whose *concept is always constant* but whose *value varies* according to the individual situation. Every population, for example, has a point of central tendency which is commonly known as the average or the mean. That *concept* of a population mean is the same for any population. But the numerical value of that mean—or average—will doubtless vary from population to population.

Take all the graduates of a certain college. They will have an average income, an average number of children, an average mortgage indebtedness on their homes, an average number of books in their personal libraries. The *idea*—the *concept*—of the *mean* will be the same for the graduates of any college, but the *value* of that mean—the *number* of children, the *amount* of family income, of home indebtedness, the *number* of books—would vary from college to college or from class to class of alumni within the same college.

The radius of a circle is a parameter of the circle. In *concept* it is a *constant* (*always* the distance from the center of the circle to the circumference) but in *numerical value*, it *varies* with each individual circle. Area is likewise a parameter, as are growth, weight, ambient temperature, atmospheric pressure.

Statistics whose function is to *describe* or *indicate* the several parameters common to all populations is that branch of parametric statistics known as *descriptive statistics*. We shall now look at some of the parameters which form the subject matter of descriptive statistics.

WHERE IS THE CENTER OF IT ALL?

When facts come to us, willy-nilly, from the environment, the first thing to do is to give those facts some organization. We need to comprehend them in some systematic manner. One of the best ways of doing this is to describe the facts. But we cannot just describe. We must describe *in terms of other factors.*

Think of it this way. A two-ton truck drives up before your home and dumps into the street a two-ton load of bricks. Another truck follows and dumps beside the bricks a two-ton load of sand. A third truck follows the second and dumps beside the sand a two-ton load of coarse limestone. You go out to survey the three piles. Each is different.

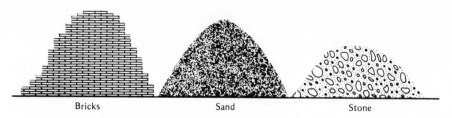

Bricks   Sand   Stone

THREE PILES OF BUILDING MATERIALS: EACH IS DIFFERENT—STATISTICALLY

You wish to *describe* the characteristics of each of these piles. You can do it in two ways: by *words* or by *statistics*. For the pile of bricks you might use such *words* as "scattered," "haphazard," "unorganized," and so forth, and these words would not tell you very much. Their power for specific communication of information would be low. On the other hand, you might describe this pile of bricks *statistically*. And to do so, you would be able to indicate the point of central equilibrium—the point at which, if you were able to split the pile at that point and to put each part on a scale, each would precisely balance the other. Then, you could actually *count* the bricks on each side and you would then have a numerically *specific* and *descriptive* fact, indicating the exact center of gravity of that pile of bricks. But this would be a cumbersome way of doing it. What you would be finding empirically would be what statisticians and researchers refer to as *the point of central tendency*. That is, the *central point* toward which all the "forces" of weight and gravity within the mass *tend* to come to rest so that a perfect balance—a static equilibrium—results.

But we cannot count all data as one might count bricks. By employing statistical procedures, therefore, we can find the point of central tendency with relatively little difficulty. The analogy of the pile of bricks is, however, appropriate.

Consider any aggregate of facts—any accumulation of data—as having certain intrinsic qualities the same as a brick has. A brick has weight; it has also extension—linear dimension. Facts also have a tendency to aggregate haphazardly much as bricks do. With the student, cited some pages back[2] who received six grades on successive tests, we have a small accumulation of data. Each grade within that accumulation is an integral unit, as each brick within the pile was an integral unit. And the center of gravity—*the point of central tendency*—within the array of accumulated grades is similar to the center of gravity within the pile of bricks. To find that "factual center of gravity" we employ so-called *measures of central tendency* which are determined statistically. There are several of these because for any one mass of data there are *several* "centers of central tendency." Think of the following rectangle as a mass of accumulated data. Note that there are several points that may be considered loci of mass equilibrium.

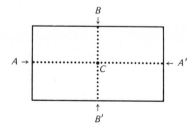

---

[2] See page 94.

We may support the rectangle at its precise center of total equilibrium—designated in the drawing as point C. On the other hand, an axis passing through the rectangle from the midpoint on the left vertical side to the midpoint on the right vertical side—designated in the drawing as A ↔ A′—would provide another kind of equilibrium. It would perfectly balance each of the horizontal halves of the rectangle. Again, were we to pass an axis through the rectangle from midpoint on the horizontal top side to the midpoint of the horizontal bottom side, we would create still another kind of equilibrium, making the vertical halves of the rectangle perfectly balanced. This axis is designated B ↔ B′ in the drawing. Thus, *the point of central tendency may mean various types of equilibrium, depending upon what we are measuring—and for what purpose.*

But, back to the *statistical* measures of central tendency. Of these measures, there are three principal types:

> The mean
> The median
> The mode

All three of these seek to find within the data that point where equilibrium occurs. We shall discuss each of these, indicating the use of each and its special ability to indicate the point of central tendency in its own way.

The mean. We can balance the mass of an object or, by the same token, a mass of data so that the *weight* of it will be equally distributed on each side of the point of equilibrium. When we so measure accumulations of data in this way, we call the point of central tendency the *mean.* Go back to the rectangle diagram. The mean would correspond to point *C* as we there indicated it.

The *common mean*, also known as the *arithmetic mean*, is found very simply by adding up all the values and dividing the sum of these by the number of the values in the series. In statistical shorthand, the arithmetic mean is frequently designated by the symbol $\overline{X}$.

Take the student's scores which we considered earlier, on page 94. Since we will be finding the arithmetic mean of these scores, think of them as *weight values* (not to be confused with *weighted scores*, which are quite different). We measure weight in degrees of heaviness: from the lightest object to the heaviest in a series. So with the student's scores. Think of the lowest score that the student earned as the *lightest*, the highest score as the *heaviest*.

Now, we shall rearrange the scores on page 94 in a series from the "lightest" score, 73, to the "heaviest," 96. The scores will then form the following series.

$$73, 79, 88, 88, 92, 96.$$

Of these scores, we shall find the arithmetic mean by adding them together and dividing the sum of the scores by 6, the number of scores in the series:

$$73 + 79 + 88 + 88 + 92 + 96 = 516 \div 6 = 86$$

The arithmetic mean is 86. That is the precise midpoint where the "weight" of the scores *below* that point exactly balance the weight of the scores *above* that point.

Test it. Subtract the two scores below the mean, 73 and 79, from 86. The difference of the first subtraction is –13; of the second –7. These scores are minus because they are *below* (i.e. *less* than) the mean.

Now, find the difference of the four scores above the mean from the mean: 88, 88, 92, and 96. These scores will be "plus" scores, since they "weigh" *more* than the mean. Their excesses are respectively 2, 2, 6, and 10. Now add the differences, those below and those above the mean:

$$-13 + -7 = -20.$$
$$2 + 2 + 6 + 10 = 20.$$

Thus, the mean stands as a fulcrum point exactly balancing the data mass on either side of it. We should, perhaps, point out that the mean in this, and in many other instances, is a *hypothetical value.* The student had no such score in the series. The mean is frequently a statistical figment of the imagination, an imaginary construct, (See p. 95.) from which to consider the entire mass of the data.

We have been discussing only *one* mean—the *arithmetic* mean. This particular mean is appropriate to indicate the point of central tendency within those data that are more or less symmetrical: data which may, when graphed, assume broadly the configurational shape of the normal (or bell-shaped) curve.[3] The normal curve depicts data which, as a whole, have characteristics of a symmetrical distribution, of equilibrium, of stability, and of balance.

But all data do not arrange themselves with such a configurational uniformity. Data differ as broadly in their integral nature and configurational profiles as do the contours and textures of those bricks, and the sand, and the stone that hypothetically you discovered in the street before your home. To appreciate this fact, go back to chapter 4. Look at the various graphical profiles of various data there.

Compare the dynamic curves of growth[4] and the whimsical saw-toothed line of hurricane wind velocity;[5] study the plummeting line of unequal economic status[6] with the perfectly reposed normal curve.[7]

Because data are so varied in their molar characteristics, we need more than one mean to locate accurately the point of equilibrium within their several masses. For that reason, we have several means other than the *arithmetic mean.* We shall look at some of these to try to understand their reason for being.

Take the phenomenon of growth. Forget, now, about statistics and think instead of the way in which growth takes place—biologically. What happens? We begin with a single cell. That cell divides into two cells; those two cells each divide into two, that makes four cells; each of these four divide into two, making eight, and so the division of cell growth proceeds: 1, 2, 4, 8, 16, 32, 64, 128, 256 and on and on. This is a mathematical series which is known as a *geometric progression.* Each following number is obtained by multiplying the preceding number by the same factor. Because of the structure of the cell, this factor in the process of growth is ordained to increase by a multiple of 2. Schematically, growth looks like this:

---

[3] See page 39.
[4] See pages 36, 38, 43, 45ff.
[5] See page 40.
[6] See page 41.
[7] See page 39.

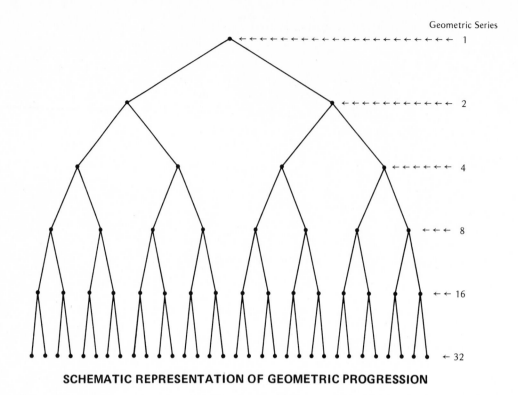

SCHEMATIC REPRESENTATION OF GEOMETRIC PROGRESSION

Quite to the contrary, the decay process is precisely the reverse of the growth progression, and the same geometric series, only in reverse or descending order, describes it: 32, 16, 8, 4, 2, 1, ½, ¼, ... So that, for both growth and decay processes, a different statistical relationship applies than that which applies to the normal curve. Perhaps the statistical expression of the fact of growth is seen most dramatically when the same process as that illustrated above is expressed in the form of a line graph. (See illustration p. 101.)

Have you seen a curve like this before? Turn to page 38. What we have graphed here is the phenomenon of cell mitosis—of the growth process. What you find on page 45 is the growth of a nation's population. The point is: they are strikingly alike. Growth produces curves like that. But behind the curve is the generic nature of the data, and the data resulting from growth phenomena will never form a normal curve. For that reason, we need a different statistical approach to locate the point of central tendency in data of this kind. For growth situations, therefore, we use a measure of central tendency known as the *geometric mean*. The computation of the geometric mean is somewhat involved, and we will not explain here how it is derived. That would be beyond the purpose of this text. Throughout this section on statistical tools, we shall refrain from complicating the explanation by presenting formulas or entering into a discussion of the manner in which the various statistical techniques are derived. That is the province of a text in statistics and beyond the needs of those who merely wish to read research and understand it. It is important in reading research, however, to be able to determine whether the researcher has, for instance, employed the proper statistical procedure to measure the characteristics of the data. And, in assessing *growth* situations, those characteristics of the data are decidedly *geometrical* rather than arithmetical. It is appropriate, therefore, to employ the *geometric mean* in locating the point of central tendency in such situations rather than any other measure of central tendency.

We have two additional forms of the mean, perhaps much less used than the forms we

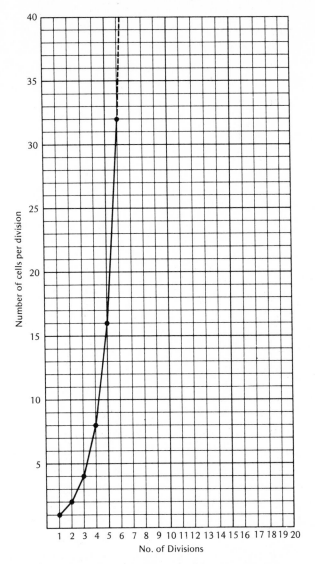

LINE GRAPH OF GEOMETRIC PROGRESSION

have just been discussing. These are: the *harmonic mean* and the *contraharmonic mean*. The *harmonic mean* is used in situations where the data fluctuate or have varying degrees of amplitude. Page 40 will describe the conditions in which the harmonic mean is appropriate. And one of the classic explanations of the harmonic mean was written nearly half a century ago and published in the *Journal of the American Statistical Association.*[8] As the author says, "The principal use of the harmonic mean is in certain cases of averaging rates." But it should be remembered that the harmonic mean cannot be employed for the average of any distribution where the variable, even in one instance, takes the value zero. We cannot average the rate of a car traveling from one point to another at a variable rate of speed if that car stops at a stop light and waits for it to change to green.

---

[8] Wirth F. Ferger, "The Nature and Use of the Harmonic Mean," *Journal of the American Statistical Association*, XXVI (March, 1939), 36-40.

The second of the lesser-used forms of the mean is the *contraharmonic mean*. This is employed in averaging such situations as that cited on pages 40 and 41. The curve that we have drawn to represent this situation is a type known as a *skewed curve*. A skewed curve throws the balance associated with the normal curve out of equilibrium. Obviously, the inordinately high salaries of a very few people in the Silica Sand and Glass Company would present an atypical picture of the "average" salary of the "average" employee, when that average is computed by the arithmetic mean. The arithmetic average would shift the salary of all the employees in the direction of the well-paid few, thus presenting an atypical situation. Figured by the contraharmonic mean, which sums the *squares* of each salary and then divides these by the sum of all the salaries, this particular mean presents a more realistic picture of the actual situation and counterbalances the effect of the small, but powerful, upward pull of the inordinately large administrative payroll.

But we have been discussing only *one* measure of central tendency: the mean. We have at least two others: the *median*, and the *mode*.

The median. We should recognize that not all *measures* of central tendency *measure* the same dimension. Each measure of central tendency measures differently, presents a different concept of the central point of the data under consideration.[9] We have the same situation in the nonstatistical world: a scale measures mass—a pound of meat, a ton of coal, a gram of a chemical compound. But a scale is useless in measuring the length of a room or the dimensions of a building lot. For that, you need a foot rule, a yardstick, a linear tape. You are evaluating a distinctly different dimension. Just so, each statistical measure evaluates a different aspect of the data.

As we have suggested earlier,[10] the *mean* is a type of fulcrum that balances the entire mass, or weight, of the data. The *median*, on the other hand, measures the central point of *extension*. It attempts to locate the *central point* which is equidistant from each end. To find the median, the data must be linear and ordinal. That is, they must be arranged in a series beginning with the least (or greatest) value and progress sequentially to the opposite end of the scale: the greatest (or least) value, as the case may be.

You recall on page 98 we discussed a student's scores which were as follows:

$$73, 79, 88, 88, 92, 96$$

If we were to find the median *value* in that series of scores, we would locate the point where as many scores lay on one side of the point as on the other. There are six scores. Obviously three must lie on one side, three on the other. The point precisely midway between scores three and four would be the median point. In this case, it would be between 88 and 88, and since there is no other value between 88 and 88, except 88, then the median would be for this series 88.

For example:

$$73 \quad 79 \quad 88 \quad 88 \quad 92 \quad 96$$

86   88

The mean ——| |—— The median

---

[9] See page 97. In that figure we may consider *C* as the mean, and *B–B'* as the median of the rectangle.
[10] See pp. 98–99.

Here we have a comparison of the median and the arithmetic mean. Note that the median is precisely in the middle of the series. That is what *median* means: it derives from the Latin, *medius,* meaning middle. We may define the median as *the value of the middle item in a series when the data are arranged in an increasing or a decreasing order of magnitude.*

What, then is the value of the median over the mean, if both of them are measures of centrality? The median has one very favorable quality: it is not easily affected by extreme values; but in problems of inference (estimation, prediction and so forth), usually met in *inferential statistics,* the mean is perhaps more trustworthy than the median.

The median belongs to a group of statistical descriptions which are commonly known as *fractiles. A fractile is a value below which lies a given fraction of a set of data.* [11] The fraction in the case of the median is, of course, ½. When we come to the discussion of measures of dispersion, we will be discussing *quartiles, deciles,* and *percentiles* which divide the range of data into fourths, tenths, and hundredths respectively.

The mode. The last, and perhaps the grossest measure of central tendency which we will discuss is the *mode.* The *mode* is defined merely as *the score that occurs most frequently in the distribution.* In the array of scores which we cited on the preceding page as illustrating the mean and the median, the score of 88 (which occurs twice) would be the mode. There are several instances where the employment of the mode might be appropriate. First, it is the easiest of the measures of central tendency to compute. Mere inspection will reveal the score which occurs with the greatest frequency. You will recall our discussion of the various types of data. [12] The mode is most commonly used when nominal data are being described. A teacher has thirty pupils in her class. Of these, three have the first name of John; two, the surname of Smith. These are nominal data. The mode of the given names would be the three Johns; that of the surnames, the two Smiths. Or, the class may be bimodal, if we consider the *entire* name of each pupil.

At times data are of such character that two or more scores occur more frequently than any others in the distribution. In such cases, we have a bimodal or polymodal distribution, as the case may be. Here, for example, are the amounts that eleven solicitors brought in from a canvass for a community project:

$107 $125 $125 $133 $146 $150 $150 $150 $167 $174 $185

There are, of course, *two* modes in this series: $125 and $150, and we call such a distribution a *bimodal distribution.*

Perhaps the appropriateness of the particular measure for the specific data may be best represented if all that we have discussed thus far were reduced to tabular form. The cardinal rule with statistics is that *the researcher must look first at the data and, then, considering the nature of the data, must choose the statistic to fit the data, and not the other way around.* For certain data, certain statistical measures are appropriate. Here, we have summarized them.

_____

[11] John E. Freund, *Modern Elementary Statistics,* third edition. Englewood Cliffs, N. J.: Prentice-Hall, Inc., p. 48.

[12] See page 71.

THE MEASURES OF CENTRAL TENDENCY

Kinds of Data			
Nominal	Ordinal	Interval	Ratio
Mode	Mode Median	Mode Median Arithmetic Mean	Mode Median Arithmetic Mean Geometric Mean Harmonic Mean Contraharmonic Mean

HOW BROAD IS THE SPREAD?

In this book, we have said some very basic things. One of these statements has been that research is merely a way of looking at life. Another is that statistics is a language that we use to describe the facts of life as we observe them. From these brief synopses, let us proceed one step further. Two facts of life are so obvious that they need no comment:

1. Everything has a center.
2. Everything extends outward, or spreads, from that center.

Statistics merely recognizes these self-evident truths and uses the language of numbers to articulate them in a different way.

The first of these propositions we have been discussing under the statistical rubric of "measures of central tendency." The second we call "measures of variability."

Variability is a fact of life. Compare any two leaves upon the same tree. They are different—they vary—from each other. Look at yourself in a mirror, one eye is higher than the other; your hands, your feet differ, one from the other. Even with machines that stamp out duplicates or presses that print copies of the same text, we find variation. Variety may not necessarily be the spice, but it most assuredly is a fact of life.

In attempting to understand, to comprehend the facts that we have observed, we need to see them, not only in terms of where their dead center lies, but also in terms of how broadly they extend or spread from that center. Go back to the pile of bricks, sand, and marbles. What you note is that each has a different contour, each has a different spread. We shall measure the spread of the data in several ways, and we shall do this only for the purpose of comprehending what the data look like when they are communicated to us through the language of statistics. The grossest measure of variability is the *range*.

The range. The range merely means the total extension of the data. If we have a series of numbers from 1 to 10, the range is from 1 to 10. It is of value in giving us some concept of the outer limits of the universe of data with which we are dealing. The range of the student's grades that we considered in the previous section was from 73 to 96, or a range of 23 grade points. We arrived at this by simple subtraction. Some statisticians, however, prefer to consider the range the difference between the lowest score and the highest score *plus 1*.

It should be recognized that the range is not a very useful measure of variation. Its main virtues are that it is simple to calculate, and it is of value in getting a quick—though not a very sophisticated—concept of data dispersion. One of the greatest criticisms of the range is its instability. Consider this series: 2, 5, 6, 7, 9, 40. The range here is from 2, the lowest figure, to 40, the highest score, but it is a somewhat spurious concept since the extreme disparity of the last figure from the rest of the series throws the whole series into instability.

The quartile deviation or the semi-interquartile range. The quartile deviation divides the entire range into four equal parts: Q_1 is that point below which 25 percent of the cases fall. Q_2 is frequently called the *semi-interquartile range*, or the point below which 50 percent of the cases fall. In this respect it compares favorably with the median in the measures of central tendency. Q_3, the third quartile, is that point below which 75 percent of the cases fall.

In the following histogram, showing the inches of monthly rainfall for a given area, we have indicated the quartiles. That area between the first and third quartile is known as the *interquartile range*. It is also interesting to note that the second quartile and the median are identical.

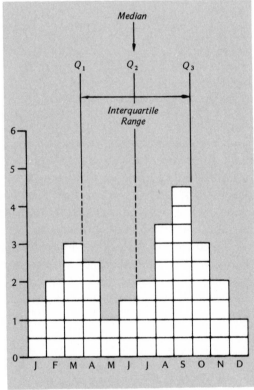

THE QUARTILE DEVIATION

The semi-interquartile range is appropriate where gross divisions are sought, in which, for instance, a teacher desires to know what students are in the upper quarter, the third quarter, the second quarter or the lower quarter of the class. It is also appropriate in distributions of data which are radically asymmetric. Wherever the median is preferred to the mean, it is safe to conclude that the semi-interquartile range is appropriate for measuring variation.

The average deviation. The semi-interquartile range is an imprecise measure of variability. If we wish to know precisely how far to the right or the left of the mean of a distribution the data are scattered, we must use a different measure to determine that fact. That measure may be either one of two: *the average deviation* or *the standard deviation*. Here we shall discuss *the average deviation.*

Assume that we have a pile of sand and a pile of marbles. They have distinctly different contours, but they have the same mean.

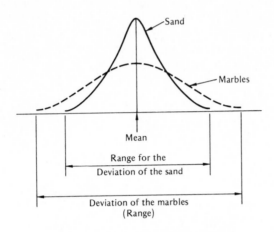

DEVIATION, RANGE, AND MEAN

Now, we see that the mean is a point of reference and that the spread of both sand and marbles can be measured *away from the mean* in either direction to determine the total spread. Instead of sand and marbles let us think of these two contours as representing numerical data, for example, the grades of students in two tests. The contours might be similar, the sand representing the grades on one test; the marbles, those on the other test. We would see the same *deviation* of academic ability which, conceivably, might form the same contours. *The average deviation* is the *average* that all of the units *deviate* from the *mean*.

We shall simplify this. Below are the student's grades that we cited on page 94, but arranged somewhat differently. They fall either above or below the mean. The mean in this case is purely a *statistical construct*—a *hypothetical value*. In the range of the student's scores, it does not exist.

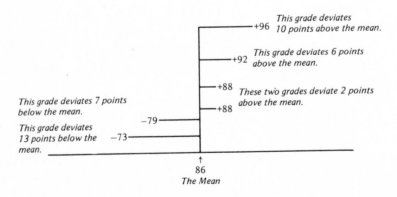

DEVIATION AROUND THE MEAN

106

Now, let's *average* all of the points (degrees) of deviation *from the mean* (disregarding the + and − signs!):

$$13 + 7 + 2 + 2 + 6 + 10 = 40 \div 6 = 6.6666+ = 6.7$$

That is, the *average* that these grades deviate from the mean is 6.7 points.

But, we have done a very unorthodox thing in *disregarding* the + and − signs. Mathematicians and statisticians frown on such behavior. And, because the average deviation engages in such a questionable practice, it is seldom used. But the theory of it is sound. What we need is to get rid of the minus values. If all values could be made positive, then they could be added and all would be well. There is one way to change a negative number to a positive one: *square it!* Multiply it by itself. That is precisely what statisticians did: they *squared each of the deviations.* That *standardized* them—it made them all positive. And the deviation that resulted from their avoidance of negative numbers, has become known as the *standard deviation.* Now, add all of these squared deviations and divide them by the total *number* of deviations, and you will have an *average* of the squared deviations. One problem remains: how do we undo what was originally done in squaring the number? No problem here: we merely take the *square root.* As a result, we have a deviation—which in itself is an *average* of all the original individual deviations from the mean—which, as we have indicated, we call the *standard deviation.*[13] It is sometimes referred to as the *root mean square.*

Perhaps at this point, we should take a moment to make some corollary matters clear. We have been discussing means and deviations. In reading research, you will soon be aware of the symbols for these measurements—and they differ, for we have *four* types of means and *four* types of deviations. In practice, researchers take only a small *sample* of a much larger *universe* or *population of data.*[14] A sanitary engineer who wishes to test the purity of the water from a well cannot, obviously, test *all* the water in the well and, in lieu of that, takes *samples* on the assumption that they represent reasonably accurately the quality of the water in the well generally. Were he to take an *average* of the bacteria found in the samples from this well and in samples of water from several other wells in neighboring locations, he would have an average derived from a number of samples, or a *sample average* or *sample mean.* This fact is important when we come to the matter of inferential statistics and the prediction of population means from sample means. We need, therefore, two symbols to identify the mean: one for the sample mean, and one for the population mean. The same holds true for the standard deviation, for we sometimes try to predict the standard deviation of the population from the standard deviation of the sample. Incidentally, any value derived from a sample is known technically as a *statistic* (not to be confused with the *plural* form of the word which is a branch of mathematics whose function is to describe facts mathematically and to test hypotheses, make estimations and predictions). The following will give you the conventional statistical symbols employed for various parameters, both those of the sample and those of the total population.

---

[13] Using the same data that we used to compute the average deviation, we shall now follow the directions for the standard deviation and compute it, by comparison.

$$\text{S.D.} = \frac{(13)^2 + (7)^2 + (2)^2 + (2)^2 + (6)^2 + (10)^2}{169 + 49 + 4 + 4 + 36 + 100} = \frac{362}{6} = 60.3. \quad \sqrt{60.3} = 7.8$$

It is seen that the average deviation and the standard deviation differ by a small margin.

[14] See page 11.

The Parameter Designated		The Symbol Used for The Sample	The Symbol Used for The Population
The Mean:	Arithmetic	$\overline{X}$	μ
	Geometric	G	
	Harmonic	H	
	Contraharmonic	CM	
Deviations:	Average	AD	
	Standard	s	σ
	From the Arithmetic Mean	x	
	The Quartile or Semi-interquartile Range	Q, Q_1, Q_2, Q_3	
Symbols of Other Measures:			
	The Median	Med	
	The Mode	Mo	
	Number or Total	n	N

Having arrived at this point in our discussion, let us look at a typical array of data as you might find them in a professional journal. Recently, an exploratory study was conducted to determine how three groups interested in sociology had obtained accurate information about older people. The instrument consisted of a test of 25 items whose answers were verified through research. The population for the study consisted of 87 undergraduate students in a class in Introductory Sociology at Duke University, and 44 graduate students and 11 faculty members in the field of human development at Duke University and Pennsylvania State University. Here were the results of the test as reported.[15]

FACTS ON AGING SCORES FOR UNDERGRADUATES, GRADUATES, AND FACULTY

Group	N	Mean % Right Answers	Standard Deviation
Undergraduate students	87	65	11.2
Graduate students	44	80	7.5
Faculty	11	90	7.7

From this table certain facts are obvious:

1. Approximately twice as many undergraduates were tested as graduates, and four times as many graduates as faculty.

---

[15] Erdman Palmore, "Facts on Aging," *The Gerontologist*, Vol. 17 (August 1977), pp. 315–320.

The critical reader of research might well question what effect, if any, this imbalance in the segments of the population might have had on the results as reported.

2. The Duke undergraduate students in Introductory Sociology classes had only two-thirds of the facts correct, compared with 80 percent correct among the graduate students in human development (at Duke University and Pennsylvania State University), and 90 percent correct among faculty in human development (at Duke and Pennsylvania State).

    The critical reader may also have additional questions and reservations at this point: Why was the population drawn from two different academic areas (sociology and human development)? Why not graduate students in sociology and faculty from sociology? Why, in the case of the graduate students and faculty was the population drawn from two universities (Duke and Pennsylvania State)? Should not the undergraduate population have also been selected in equal proportion from the two universities? Does this introduce a bias factor in favor of or prejudicial to the undergraduate group? [Review pp. 74-80 for a discussion of bias.] How were the students and faculty chosen for this study? With respect to the faculty, was any attempt made to equalize that segment of the population? (A full professor having taught human development for 20 years and having an interest in aging—perhaps because of his own age—is quite different from an instructor or assistant professor who has taught but a few years and has little interest in the problems of aging.)

3. The standard deviation column indicates the *average* spread of the test scores. The scores of the undergraduate students had approximately a 33 percent broader spread—between the lowest score and the highest score—than those of the graduate students and the faculty. There was little difference of the average spread of the scores around the mean for the faculty and graduate students.

    The critical reader may be interested in the cause for the broad deviation from the mean for the undergraduate students. Undergraduates in Introductory Sociology are generally freshmen or sophomores and as a group may have both little interest and little knowledge with respect to aging. Graduate students and faculty, on the other hand, may have had courses in problems of the aging and not only more knowledge but a developed interest in the subject. The author indicates that one purpose of the study was "to measure and compare different groups' overall level of information about aging." This goal seems to have been achieved. But the great disparity in the character and composition of the groups still leaves questions that should be resolved.

The above observations and reactions may be those of the reader of research who would look at the table and react to its data. We present it here to illustrate what it means to read research, and particularly to read the statistics of research *critically*.

Since the normal curve demonstrates both the measures of central tendency and the measures of dispersion, and since it features so prominently in the measures of prediction and estimation, which we will consider somewhat later in this chapter, we present it here with its major statistical implications.

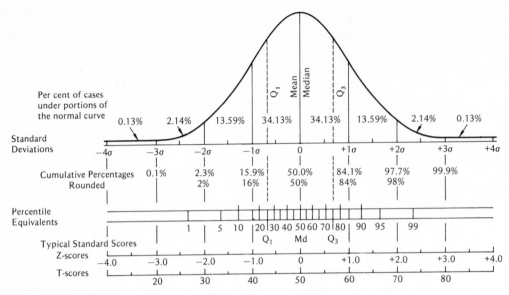

STATISTICAL IMPLICATIONS OF THE NORMAL CURVE

If we study the normal curve and its various properties, we will find that it is an illustration of much that we have discussed thus far. First, we should note that the data noted are predicated upon a perfect, normal distribution. This is an ideal distribution. At the very center of the curve, dividing it exactly in half, are the mean and the median. Lying on either side of this central location are the first and the third quartiles. Between them lie 50 percent of the data. Further out, we have the first standard deviation from the mean. Within this area lie 68.26 percent of the data. This is approximately 2/3 of the data. If, for example, we have 100 grades on a test *and the distribution of the scores form a normal distribution*, then approximately two-thirds of the grades will fall on either side of the mean (median) within the first standard deviation. Lying further away is the area of the second standard deviation, *on either side of the mean*. If what we consider the large "average" group of scores fan out on either side of the mean 34.13 percent, or a total of 68.26 percent, then 13.59 percent of the scores will lie *below* this group and 13.59 percent *above* this group. The tails of the curve embrace the last two standard deviations with 2.14 percent at each end in the third standard deviation area and 0.13 percent in the area of the fourth deviation. Should your instructor decide to grade his papers "on the curve," these are the proportions of distribution that he would probably use. Roughly two-thirds of the grades would be C, 13 to 14 percent would be B and D grades, and 2 to 3 percent would be F and A grades.

If, on the other hand, you take a standardized test and learn that your placement on that test was at the 80th percentile, it means that you placed at the upper end of the first standard deviation above the mean, or 30 percent above the average for the class. The percentile equivalents scale is shown just below the cumulative percentage scale on the chart above.

Now we come to the z-scores and the T-scores. You will come across reference to these scores in reading research. Both are called *standard scores*. This means that, although the raw data were in two different areas and consequently not *comparable*, by referring each score to the mean and to the standard deviation, we can by statistical computation (as to how it is done, we need not worry) resolve each one to a z- or *standard score*.

For instance, if Mary runs a track race in 13.2 minutes which has a mean of 14 minutes, and a S.D. of 5.6 minutes; if she lifts a 40-pound weight 4 feet 9 inches, for which we have comparable data of mean and standard deviation for Mary's group; and in home economics class, Mary received a grade of 87, with mean and variation available for this class also: now, by calculating the z-score, we can compare these three disparate facts. This helps us to see an across-the-board view of Mary's achievement which would not be possible without this means of converting all these scores to comparable units.

T-scores are similar to z-scores except for the fact that unlike z-scores, which use the $\overline{X}$ and s of the data distribution, T-scores standardize the data on a predetermined $\overline{X}$ of 50, and a s of 10.

FACTS, TOO, HAVE RELATIONSHIPS

So far, we have considered only a *one-dimensional aspect of the facts*. Where is the center of the data? How far do they extend on either side of the center? And, how do we measure these dimensions? To those questions we have found answers. But, we have been concerned with only *one* dimension of data and its characteristics: centrality and extension.

Now we shall look at *two* kinds of data and their relationship to each other. See life as it really is, and you will discover that facts do not always exist *alone*. Often they are related to other facts. Degrees of relationship exist among facts as degrees of relationship exist among people. These relationships may be very close, or they may be so tenuous as to be scarcely recognizable. In fact, there may be no relationship at all or a negative relationship, and all of these degrees of affinity or opposition we can determine and express statistically. *Relationship* is a fact of life and of research, and it can be measured and evaluated.

Percentages. Perhaps the simplest and the most common statistical quasirelationship is expressed by the *percentage* figure. A student makes a grade of 80 percent on a test. It is the expression of the *relationship* between the number of items correct and the total number of items in the entire test.

Many research reports present the data in the form of percent categories. Such tables of percentage values must be read with insight and with an awareness of what a percentage value actually represents.

To read percentage data intelligently, we should *always* know the *number* of individuals, or items, in the sample or population of which the percentage figure is but a fractional part. To say, for example, that the candidate received 80 percent of the votes without knowing how many voters participated in the election is to tell us nothing. There is a vast difference in an election of a president to a community organization on a snowy night when only ten members of the group were present and eight voted for the candidate, and a labor union of 100,000 members in which 80,000 voted for the candidate. In reading research involving percentages, the appropriate question to ask is always: What percent of *what*?

Responsible research reports will indicate the total population, of which the percentages are fractional parts, by the symbol N = followed by a number, thus: $N = 20$. In such a table, 70 percent represents 14 individuals or items.

Earlier in chapter three,[16] we presented a research report, "On the Tendency for Volunteer Helpers to Give Advice." In the table, summarizing the data by percentage of responses in each "response mode category," note that for each call both the sex and the number of

---

[16] See page 30.

the volunteers is given. This provides a base against which to interpret the percentage values in the six categories which follow.

Compare this presentation of data with that in the histogram below.[17] It indicates the "percentage of all students [but, *how many students* were *all* students?] reporting that they received . . . praise" from their teachers for their achievement in high school mathematics.

In addition to the fact that this histogram presents *no* numerical base against which to evaluate the percentages, note also the inaccuracy in wording which the heading displays: "Percentage of all students reporting that they . . . received praise *by high school math achievement scores*"! Language is a mirror of the mind. Reportorial haze should alert you to read the report with circumspection and with more than usual care. You have read those words before.[18] They are here appropriate.

PERCENTAGE OF ALL STUDENTS REPORTING
THAT THEY USUALLY OR ALWAYS
RECEIVED ACADEMIC PRAISE BY
HIGH-SCHOOL MATH ACHIEVEMENT SCORES

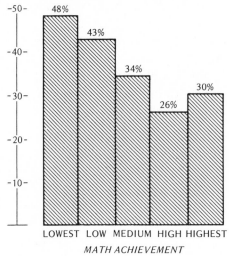

Product-moment correlation. While percentage ratios have about them *some* of the qualities of relationship, some readers may not consider percentage measurements to belong to the true correlational techniques. For that reason, we have called them *quasi*-relationships.

The most common indicator of true relationship between one mass of data and another (e.g. height-weight, age-achievement, level, temperature-pressure, environment factor-disease incidence) may be the *product-moment correlation.* This discovery of relationship is an integral part of the scientific method.[19] "The scientific method . . . consists in the careful and laborious classification of facts, *in the comparison of their relationship and sequences,*

[17] Paul Copperman, *The Literary Hoax: The Decline of Reading, Writing, and Learning in the Public Schools and What We Can Do About It.* New York: William Morrow and Company, Inc. 1978, p. [158].

[18] See page 17.

[19] See pp. 9-12.

[italics added] and finally in the discovery by the aid of disciplined imagination of a brief statement or *formula,* which in a few words resumes a wide range of facts. Such a formula . . . is termed a scientific law."[20] This was the first germinal statement of the idea which finally resulted in Karl Pearson's product–moment correlation.

To co-relate, we need two kinds of data, and we need to so arrange these data that they may express a relationship which varies from zero (no relationship) to 1.00–a perfect correspondence, identity of relationship. To do this, we employ a grid with the values (the magnitudes) of the one variable arranged along one axis and the values of the other variable arranged along the other axis.[21] On such a grid, we express one variable (one fact) in terms of the other variable (the other fact). This is such a commonplace procedure that we seldom think of it being a mathematical operation: Jane is 10 years old and is in the fifth grade. There, we have expressed Jane's age in *relation to* her academic achievement. Let's transfer that information to a grid.

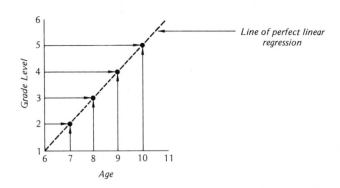

PERFECT LINEAR RELATIONSHIP

Note that the correspondence of Jane's age to her grade level is 1:1, and the resultant line that connects all of the 1:1 relationships is known as the *line of perfect linear regression.* It is a line that *regresses* from the vectors of age and grade level, which in statistics we refer to as *axis X* and *axis Y* respectively.

Consider, now, that Jane is in high school. There are twelve members in her class, and we are exploring the theory that those who have high academic achievement in English are likewise superior in foreign languages. There is, in other words, a high correlation between achievement in English and achievement in a foreign language. We would plot all twelve students' grades on a grid in the same fashion as we did above, with this exception: they will show much greater scatter and, in a sense, rotate around the axis of the line of linear regression.

Plotted on a grid, the grades of these students may appear as follows:

---

[20] Karl Pearson, *The Grammar of Science.* London: Adam and Charles Black, 1900, p. 77.
[21] See page 36 ff.

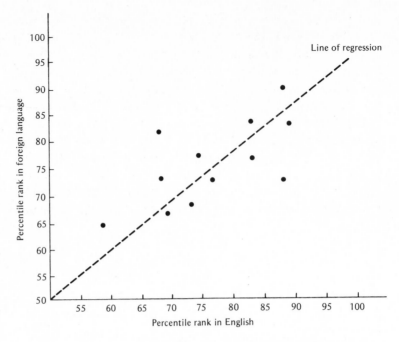

TYPICAL CORRELATIONAL MATRIX OF STUDENT'S GRADES

What we have here is a *scatter diagram*. It represents the grades of the twelve students in Jane's class as these grades lie in proximity to the line of regression. Here are the grades of these students in each subject:

English	Foreign Language
76	80
85	80
70	85
90	75
65	60
75	70
90	95
70	75
85	87
78	75
92	87
72	67

Obviously, the closer the data clusters about the regression line, the closer will be the correlation between the two variables. Correlation coefficients are indicated by the italic *r* = followed by a decimal fraction. This indicates the degree of co-relation between the variables. For the data which we have just presented *r* = .66. But what does that mean? As we pointed out earlier, positive correlations[22] may range from 0, which is no correlation,

---

[22] There is, of course, *negative* correlation, whose scale runs from 0.0 to –1.0, thus the *full* range of the Pearsonian *r* is from –1.0 to +1.0. Generally, in reading research reports, we seldom encounter negative correlation, and therefore need not discuss it further in this text.

to 1.00, which is a perfect correlation. The *degree* of correlation is, therefore, a relative matter and ranges along a sliding scale from 0.0 to 1.0. For practical purposes, and as a rule-of-thumb, .8 and above is usually considered a high coefficient of correlation, .5 is moderate, and an *r* of .3 and below is considered a low coefficient. An *r* of .66, therefore, is in the mid-range between moderate and high correlation status.[23]

In reading research, we should be wary of a mistake that is sometimes made by researchers in assuming either by overt statement or by implication that correlation and causality are the same. Even though you may have a high correlation between two variables, this in no way implies that the one variable is the cause of the other. You cannot assume, for instance, that because there is a high incidence of thunderstorms in any one year and also that there is a high incidence of female births and that these correlate at .88 that the one event is the *cause* of the other. We cannot *extrapolate* causation. In the absence of *direct and explicit evidence*, beyond the bounds of the correlation, no assumption of causality is warranted.

Before discussing other types of correlation, it may be well for us to explore why this is called the product–*moment* correlation. A moment is, of course, a word whose statistical meaning is a derivative of the mechanical usage of the word. A *moment*, in mechanics, *is the tendency to produce rotation about an axis*. That is precisely what the data appear to do in a correlation matrix such as the one we presented above. They lie on either side of the regression axis and, in a sense, seem to rotate around it.

We have, perhaps, said enough about linear correlation of two variables. There are times, however, when it is desirable to correlate a number of variables, each with the other. Such a procedure is known as *multiple correlation* and the form in which it is presented is characteristically unique as is seen here. This form of presenting correlational data is known as an *intercorrelational matrix*.

The above table presents eight variables which are correlated with each other. These eight are listed in the left hand column under the heading "Variable." The numbers above the columns from 1 to 8 refer to the same eight variables. When, for example, the mental age (MA) of the child is correlated with the mental age of the child (item 1), horizontally and vertically, we have a perfect correlation of identity (1.00). But when the mental age is correlated against the intelligence quotient (IQ), we have a very high relationship between these two factors of .92. Taking the item at the bottom of the first column: chronological age (CA) in months upon entering grade 1, we find practically no relationship between chronological age and mental age. The coefficient of correlation is .01 (negligible).

The mean and standard deviation were derived, as the author explains in the report, from a test situation in which "12 children took a test comprised of 173 words; 8 others

---

[23] Sometimes the range is fractioned further in order to gain a clearer comprehension of precisely what the *r*-decimal may mean. Here is one such scale:

.80 to 1.00 highly dependable relationship
.60 to .79 moderate to marked relationship
.40 to .59 fair degree of relationship
.20 to .39 slight relationship
.00 to .19 negligible or chance relationship.

The same interpretation would apply to negative correlations, except the relationships would be inverse.
—From Robert H. Koenker, *Simplified Statistics*. Totowa, New Jersey: Littlefield, Adams & Co., 1971, p. 52.

TABLE 2   CORRELATION MATRIX, MEANS, AND STANDARD DEVIATIONS FOR EXPERIMENTAL GROUP (N = 33) AT THE END OF THE 2-YEAR PROGRAM

	Variable	1	2	3	4	5	6	7	8
1	MA (mos.), in March	1.00							
2	IQ, in March	.92	1.00						
3	Intelligence Raw Score, in March	.94	.92	1.00					
4	No. of Letters Named, in May	.39	.46	.47	1.00				
5	No. of Numerals Named, in May	.36	.40	.41	.83	1.00			
6	No. of Words Identified, in May	.59	.57	.59	.65	.69	1.00		
7	No. of Known Sounds, in May	.56	.49	.57	.59	.70	.74	1.00	
8	CA (mos.) upon entering grade 1	.01	−.31	.02	−.14	−.06	.02	.07	1.00
	Mean	82.79	114.18	46.60	49.61	46.94	125.42	15.52	74.82
	S.D.	13.10	12.16	6.15	7.09	9.55	42.03	5.95	3.51

Value of r significant at $p < .05$ is .29 (one-tailed test).
Dolores Durkin, "Six Year Study of Children Who Learned to Read in School at the Age of Four," *Reading Research Quarterly*, Vol. 10, No. 1 (1974–1975), p. 18.

took a test of 150 words; another group of 6 took a 118-item test; the remaining 7 subjects were asked to identify 110 words. Averaging the 33 scores [Note at the head of the table N = 33], the mean was 125.4 words correctly identified."

The author continues:

Not all the experimental subjects had received concentrated instruction and practice with the 22 sounds comprising the sound test (5 short vowel sounds and 17 consonant sounds). However, all had been exposed to them in connection with writing lessons, so all were given the same test. Results are in Table 2 and indicate a mean score of 15.5 on the sound test.

When other data in Table 2 are examined, the most apparent and persistent trend is the lack of relationship between a subject's chronological age and his achievement in the various areas that were tested. This is an interesting trend because of the school's persistent use of chronological age as *the* criterion for entrance.

As in all reports that are carefully written, the author not only presents the data in statistical form but, in addition, analyzes the statistical array for the reader pointing out to the reader of the research the noteworthy features of the data presentation.

Other correlational techniques. Thus far, we have been considering only *one* of the means of correlating data. To be sure, the Pearson product-moment correlation is, by far, the most common type of correlational technique that you will meet in reading research. But the specific method of correlation must be chosen in terms of the *kind of data* which are being correlated. We have been considering, for example, a method of correlation which can be used only with data that are *continuous: both* variable *X* and variable *Y* must be continuous data. Continuous data are those connected facts that do not naturally segregate into discrete categories or dichotomies. Degrees of temperature, the range of grades on an examination, one's age, the letters of the alphabet, financial data, height, weight—all these are examples of continuous data. The Pearson product-moment correlation can use only such data. If data are of other types—dichotomous, ranked, consisting of discrete categories— then other methods of correlation must be employed.

Since these are not nearly so common as the Pearson product moment correlation, we shall merely mention them briefly, giving their principal data requirements.

TYPES OF CORRELATION, OTHER THAN THE PEARSON PRODUCT-MOMENT CORRELATION, FOUND IN RESEARCH REPORTS

Type of Correlation	Symbol	Characteristics of the Variables	Comment
Biserial correlation	r_{bis}, r_b	Values of one variable are continuous, values of the other variable dichotomous. Example: academic grades (continuous) and race: white and non-white (dichotomous).	Frequently used in item analysis. Dichotomies are usually artificial: pass–fail, succeed–nonsuccess.
Point biserial correlation	r_{pbis}, r_{pb}	One variable uses continuous data, the values of the other are discrete or truly dichotomous. Examples of true dichotomous data: yes–no, boys–girls, black–white, blonds-brunettes.	Widely used to determine the ability of an item in a test to discriminate between good and poor students.
Phi coefficient (Also known as the Four-fold Coefficient)	ϕ	Each variable is a true dichotomy. See comment under point biserial correlation for examples of true dichotomous data.	A statistic closely related to the chi square technique. May be used to test the discriminating function of a test item, or of one item among a group of items.
Tetrachoric correlation	r_t	Both variables are continuous but are categorized into dichotomies. For example, we divide a group of test papers into the passing and the failing, then we correlate with this group those answers that were right and those that were wrong.	A complex statistical procedure. Must not be used with nominal or ordinal data. Less reliable than the Pearson product-moment.
Correlation ratio	η	The data in each of the variables are continuous.	Although, like the product-moment correlation the data may be continuous in both variables, the relationship between the two sets of variables is not linear. A scattergram is necessary to determine linearity.

TYPES OF CORRELATION, OTHER THAN THE PEARSON
PRODUCT-MOMENT CORRELATION, FOUND IN RESEARCH REPORTS   (Cont.)

Type of Correlation	Symbol	Characteristics of the Variables	Comment
Spearman rank–order correlation (Rank difference correlation)	ρ	The data in both variables are arranged in ranked order.	This is a nonparametric technique. It is similar to the product-moment correlation, and is particularly well suited to correlation of situations of 25–30 cases.
Kendall's coefficient of correlation	W	This technique used with three or more sets of ranks.	To test the correspondence or agreement or disagreement between several evaluative situations. Value of W varies between 0 = no agreement to 1 = perfect agreement.
Kendall's tau-correlation between ranks	γ	Both sets of data are expressed as ranks.	Very similar to ρ but preferred when the number of cases is less than 10.
Contingency coefficient	C	Each variable is expressed as two or more categories.	This technique is very similar to r_t. It is also related to χ^2. Similar also to ϕ. For two classes (categories) r_t or ϕ may be used, for more than two categories C is appropriate.
Partial correlation	$r_{12.3}$	Two variables influenced by a third variable.	Workers are evaluated on the relationship between production time and production quality while working under adverse lighting conditions (third variable influence).
Multiple correlation	$R_{1.234}$	One variable (criterion) vs. several variables.	Employed where two or more variables are used to predict a single variable. In the symbol $R_{1.234....n}$, the subscript 1 stands for the criterion variable; the 2, 3, 4, for the predictor variables.

HOW TO USE THIS CHART IN READING RESEARCH

In reading a research report, you may come across one of these non-Pearsonian r correlations. If the author of the research report refers to it merely by symbol, the second column will help you identify the technique. If the name of the correlation technique is given, then columns 2, 3, and 4 will give you some orientation information so that you will be able to read the discussion with some knowledge of the characteristics and the use of that particular correlational approach. How these coefficients are derived is a statistical consideration and beyond the scope of this book. For those desiring to understand the statistical implications of these techniques, N. M Downie and R. W. Heath, *Basic Statistical Method*, Fourth edition, (New York: Harper & Row, 1974) will be found very helpful. A very elementary text is one by Robert H. Koenker, *Simplified Statistics for Students in Education and Psychology* (Totowa, New Jersey: Littlefield, Adams & Co., a paperback.

HOW MUCH IS DUE TO CHANCE?

We gamble on the facts. We assume that what we do *not* know is similar to what we *do* know. This process we call *prediction*. In statistics, we refer to it as *probability*. John Maynard Keynes wrote a book with the title *A Treatise on Probability*.[24] In the opening chapter of that work, Keynes says

> Part of our knowledge we obtain direct; and part by argument. The Theory of Probability is concerned with that part which we obtain by argument, and it treats of the different degrees in which the results so obtained are conclusive or inconclusive. . . . The terms *certain* and *probable* describe the various degrees of rational belief about a proposition which different amount of knowledge authorize us to entertain.[25]

This opens a new domain in the study of statistics. To this point, we have been studying those phenomena whose *totality* we can describe and evaluate. If we have a group of scores, we can find the mean, describe the spread, investigate the relationship between those scores and others that may be relevant to them.

Now we voyage into the unknown. And we must understand some basic principles in connection with this new statistical orientation.

Samples and populations. It is not long before every researcher is aware that *all* of the facts cannot be studied. For that reason, we must be content to "see" the facts through the narrow window of a few of them. These few we call a *sample.* We want to know what the Greek people are like. We visit a few cities, we talk to a few of the people, we observe a minute segment of the Greek life style: we *sample* their culture, their attitudes, their reactions. From this, we extrapolate, drawing conclusions about the Greek population as a whole. It is the only way we know how to see the many— except through the few.

Earlier[26] we mentioned the biologist who wished to determine the safety of the drinking water from the wells in a certain community. The samples that the sanitary engineer takes comprise, as Keynes says, the "part of our knowledge that we obtain direct." From these samples, we "argue" that the totality of the water content of the wells is like the samples we have just analyzed. And Keynes continues, "the theory of probability is concerned with that part which we obtain by argument."

Standard error of the mean. This brings us to a fact which every researcher must face: reality is difficult to find; consistency is a fact that nature abhors. At best, we can view the universe of data through a mere slit in the wall of our limitations that separates us from the totality of the data.

We are aware that the Japanese, in general, are a people of relatively short stature. Conversely, the Scandinavians are, as a rule, taller. We wish to know what the height and weight of the *average* American is. Obviously, we cannot go out to measure *every* adult in our population. That would be an impossible task. We must *estimate* the universe of data from an inspection of *samples* that we survey. We must view the universe of data through the slit in the wall.

The accuracy of seeing the totality of any such situation through such a small aperture as provided by a sample will depend upon two important matters:

---

[24] John Maynard Keynes, *The Collected Writings of John Maynard Keynes*, Volume 8: A *Treatise in Probability*. New York: St. Martin's Press for the Royal Economic Society, 1973.
[25] Op cit., p. 3.
[26] See page 107.

1. That the sample be as unbiased (i.e., as representative of the totality) as possible; and
2. That the samples be as nearly as possible identical to each other.

The matter of bias we discussed in earlier pages of this book.[27] But it is the matter of identity of sample that should receive some comment here. Those who have attempted sampling have discovered a very interesting and important fact: No matter how random, how representative the sample is, it will never precisely reflect the parameters of the universe of data or the population from which the sample was selected. Samples, no matter how carefully selected, are not miniature populations.

We discover this most dramatically when we look at comparable parameters, particularly the mean. If, for example, we take a college class of 1,000 students and give all of them the Graduate Record Examination, we find that the mean for the total population is 694. But, had we taken a 50% sample of the class and, selecting students as randomly as possible, we would select 5 samples of 100 students each, we may have found that on the same GRE their mean scores would have shown something like this:

Group No.	Mean Score
1	692.7
2	695.3
3	696.1
4	693.9
5	693.0

$\overline{X}$ of the sample means = 694.2, a variance of +0.2 from the population mean. We have a series of five means that rotate around the population mean. Some sample means are above, some below, but none, *identical* to the population mean. This variance of the mean, we express in terms of a statistic called the *standard error of the mean*, and it is represented by the symbol $SE_{\overline{X}}$.

We postulate, of course, that the mean of the population and those of the samples should reasonably approximate each other. Were we to gather sufficient samples, each with its shifting mean of however small degree, we would find that if the number of the samples chosen were large enough, we would approach closer and closer to the population mean. This is known as the *central limit theorem*.

In practice, however, we attack the problem from a slightly different angle. First, we set up what is known as a *null hypothesis*. A *hypothesis* is a temporary judgment. It is a position that we hold long enough to test whether it is true or untrue, whether we should accept it or reject it, whether it is valid or not.

The *null hypothesis* postulates that there is *no (null)* difference between the parameters of one set of data and those of another set of data. Incidentally, we represent this hypothesis by the symbol H_O.

But, in no situation can we be one hundred percent certain. We have seen that with individuals drawn from the same group and tested in smaller groups, the parameters (mean and standard deviation) rotate in tiny orbits around the polar value of the population mean. The question is, however, how far may those orbits stray before we lose *confidence* in their

---

[27] See pages 74-80.

ability to represent a reasonable approximation of the population parameter? When, in fact, does the *error* between the sample values and those of the population become so gross as to be a *significant error*? Where is the boundary where error ceases to be a reasonable deviation and becomes an entirely new value? These questions are important to the researcher.

It is customary, therefore, for researchers to state what *confidence interval (or range) or* what *level of significance* the data will be permitted before the variation becomes so pronounced as to demand that the null hypothesis be rejected. This is usually set at a 1 percent (.01) or a 5 percent (5.0) level of significance. If, for example, the limit is set at the .05 *level of significance,* it means that the researcher would permit a 5 percent variance, considered as being due to *pure chance.* Any variance *beyond, or in excess of, that magnitude* would be considered to be due to some other influence—aside from pure chance or natural fortuitousness—to be operating within the system and would, consequently, cause the null hypothesis to be rejected.

Level of significance is usually indicated by the symbol $p. < .05$.

But nothing is sure. Even though we reject the null hypothesis, there is a possibility that we may be rejecting the hypothesis when, indeed, it should be accepted. This is known as a *Type I error.* To avoid this, we may narrow the chance of error probability to the 1 percent $(p. < .01)$ or still further to the .1 percent level $(p. < .001)$. However, when we do this, we are running the risk of accepting the null hypothesis when, in fact, it should be rejected. This causes us to commit a *Type II error.* In practice, most researchers will tend to be cautious and try to limit the possibility of making a Type I error.

In reading research, you should remember that *significance level* called, alpha, and *interval of confidence (or confidence interval)* are complements of each other. A .05 level of significance is precisely the same as a 95 percent confidence interval. One deals with the small segment of the data which, if it extends *beyond* that limit will cause it to become suspect, and cause the rejection of the null hypothesis. The 95 percent confidence interval means that we will accept 95 percent (or more) of the data, but if extraneous influences cause it to shrink *below* the 95 percent level, we will lose *confidence* in the data and, hence, we consequently reject the hypothesis.

Note the illustration following. The *confidence interval*—that area under the distribution curve in which we can have confidence in the data that there is no (null) difference between those data and similar data from a corresponding sample—is represented by the clear area. Limiting the confidence interval, at either end of the curve, are the points of *critical value.*

We determine the *level of significance* (or confidence interval) by subjecting the data to a z or t test. When we get the z or the t statistic for the specific data which we have under consideration, we compare that statistic to a table value—called a *critical value*—to determine whether the computed value exceeds the critical value. If the computed value exceeds the critical value, the difference between the two values did not occur by pure chance and the two groups of data are significantly different. This causes the null hypothesis, which states that there will be no difference between the samples, to be rejected. Perhaps the following illustration will make this discussion meaningful.

We should point out that hypotheses of whatever sort—and this includes the null hypothesis—cannot be *proved* or *disproved.* They are merely *accepted* or *rejected* depending upon what the data indicate.

The reader of statistics should always look for two factors with respect to the data. First, the reader should determine whether a claim of significance is made, and what the

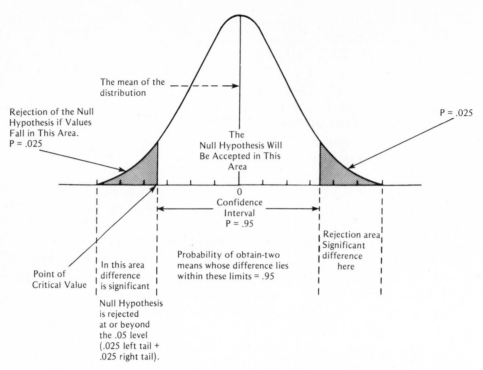

The mean of the distribution

Rejection of the Null Hypothesis if Values Fall in This Area.
P = .025

P = .025

The Null Hypothesis Will Be Accepted in This Area

0
Confidence Interval
P = .95

Point of Critical Value

In this area difference is significant

Probability of obtain-two means whose difference lies within these limits = .95

Rejection area Significant difference here

Null Hypothesis is rejected at or beyond the .05 level (.025 left tail + .025 right tail).

ACCEPTING OR REJECTING THE NULL HYPOTHESIS

level of that significance is. Secondly, the reader should observe what statistical test of the hypothesis has been made and what this test has revealed in terms of the acceptance or rejection of the hypothesis.

The whole matter of statistical tests may be somewhat sophisticated for a text of this nature. We shall, therefore, merely discuss the most common of these tests and indicate the situations in which they are most commonly employed. Perhaps to feel perfectly at home in this area, a much more thorough incursion into inferential statistics may be in order. To give you an introduction, however, we shall outline briefly the principal tests of hypotheses which are commonly encountered in reading research. The reason for these tests is that the observed phenomena will not agree completely with those expected by the null hypothesis. We must be prepared, therefore, to accept some variance from the ideal; we must be willing to concede that we will be tolerant enough to allow some margin of error—and this is where the level of significance becomes critical—in making a decision as to whether we shall accept or reject the null hypothesis.

We can classify the principal tests in several categories depending upon either the nature of the data or the character of the parameter. First, we are interested in the parameters of the mean and the standard deviation.

Z tests and t tests. The Z tests are used when we have (1) only one variable; (2) a random sample; (3) the number of units in the sample—the size of the sample—is more than 30 units. These tests are employed in three principal situations, and we shall detail them below:

1. When the *standard deviation (σ) of the population* and the *population mean (μ) are known, the Z* test is used to test whether the *mean of a chosen sample* differs significantly from the *population mean.*

2. When we know only the *standard deviation of the sample (s)* and the *population mean (μ)*, the Z test should be employed to test whether the *sample mean* is significantly different from the *population mean.* In this, we must assume that the standard deviation of the sample is a reasonable estimate of the standard deviation of the population.

3. A *comparison* can be made between *samples* to determine whether there is any significant difference between a sample taken from different segments of the same population. We compare the intelligence of children from an urban area with those from a rural area to determine whether there is any significant difference between the IQ's of the two samples.

The t test, sometimes known as Student's t, was developed in 1908 by W. S. Gosset (1876-1937), a statistician in the employ of the Guinness brewery. The policy of the firm forbade its employees to publish research. Gosset circumvented this regulation by publishing his statistical formula for the evaluation of small samples under the pseudonym of "Student." Hence, the test became known as "Student's t."

The t distribution is used with samples numbering less than 30 units. In this sense, it becomes a complementary test to the Z test, which is appropriate for populations of *more* than 30 units.

In reading research in which the t test is employed, you will doubtless encounter a concept known as *degrees of freedom*, abbreviated *df.* This is usually defined as one *less* than the number of units in the sample $(n - 1)$. Thus, if a sample consisted of 10 units, it would have 9 degrees of freedom. Degrees of freedom are also commonly used with the chi-square distribution, which we will discuss later. The t test is always cited for t values at the .05 and the .01 level of significance, with the appropriate number of degrees of freedom.

Graphed, the t distribution is very similar to the contour of the normal curve.

The chi-square (χ^2) *test.* The χ^2 test usually involves the use of a *contingency table*, sometimes referred to as a 2×2 or 2×3 *contingency table*, depending upon the number of "cells" that it contains. Perhaps an example of a contingency table will be the best way to understand what it is. It is the representation of categorical data and the frequencies associated with those data. We have two teams, the Red Team and the White Team. We are listing the number of games each team won, and those they lost. Set into a contingency table these data would appear as follows:

	Games Won	Games Lost
Red Team	12	6
White Team	10	8

The primary use of the χ^2 statistic is to show the degree of divergence between the observed and the expected frequencies. This is generally called the *goodness of fit* between theory and fact. We wish to compare the grades of a class with the expected frequencies that one might expect from the normal curve distribution. χ^2 will indicate how well the grades of the class "fit" the expected contour of the normal frequency distribution. If the observed frequencies deviate markedly from the expected normal distribution it may indicate that some influence was at work (the students were not taught as thoroughly as they should have been; they were not a class of "normal" academic ability—the class contained a large number of exceptional children, and so forth). We might use the χ^2 to provide a departure point from which to look for causes extraneous to the data under scrutiny.

The χ^2 test, it should be noted, is a *nonparametric test* and, as such, it can be used in situations where the common parametric tests are incapable of functioning. For example, instead of the smooth normal curve of the parametric world, with its mean, median, standard deviations, and other parametric landmarks, we have the dichotomous world of good-bad, is–is not, up–down and similar extreme differences. We also have a categorical world of classes. Where data come to us in these forms, the χ^2 statistic is an appropriate evaluative technique. It is extremely valuable in causal comparative studies, where we have a comparison between observed and theoretical frequencies, or where we may have two variables from independent samples, each of which may be categorized in two ways. Chi square is also valuable in analyzing data which have been expressed in frequencies rather than as measurement data. Chi square is furthermore used in *tests of independence*—that is, for the significance of the difference between two or more groups to certain characteristics when those groups have been classified into categories. An interesting application of this use of χ^2 was made at the University of California, Los Angeles, Hospital to test the theory (and widely-held old-wives'-tale belief) that more children are born at the time of full moon than at other times of the lunar cycle. The study appeared in a brief communication to *The New England Journal of Medicine.*[28]

HUMAN BIRTHS AND THE PHASE OF THE MOON

To the Editor: It is widely believed that human births occur most frequently at the time of the full moon; the belief is prevalent even among nurses at maternity wards. Of published studies of the frequency of births as a function of period in the lunary cycle, however, some[1]

Table 1. Probability of Random Selection of a Sample Differing More than the University of California, Los Angeles, Hospital Sample from a Population in Which the Birthrate is Uniform throughout the Cycle of Lunar Phases.

Group and Sample Size	Chi-Square	Degrees of Freedom	Probability
All live births — 11,691	17.91	29	0.95
Natural births — 8,142	25.64	29	0.65
Multiple births — 141	7.24	5	0.20
Still births — 168	2.48	5	0.78

show negative results, and others[2-4] show weak positive correlations that are inconsistent with each other.

We have analyzed the distribution of all births at the University of California, Los Angeles, Hospital during 51 lunar cycles from March 17, 1974, through April 30, 1978. During this period, there were 11,691 live births, of which 8142 were natural (not induced by drugs or cesarean

[28] George O. Abell and Bennett Greenspan, "Human Births and the Phase of the Moon," *The New England Journal of Medicine*, Vol. 300, No. 2 (January 11, 1979), p. 96.

section). The live births included 141 multiple sets (136 sets of twins, four of triplets and one of quadruplets). In addition, there were 168 stillbirths. Thus, we have four samples: all live births, natural live births, multiple births and stillbirths.

In no sample was the mean number of births occurring on the date of the full moon above average. We used the standard chi-square test to calculate the probability that each sample was a random selection from a population in which all types of birth occur with uniform frequency throughout the lunar cycle. Table 1 shows that in none of the samples is there reason to reject the hypothesis of the random selection. We conclude that the birthrate at this hospital during the period surveyed does not correlate in any way with the cycle of lunar phases (we shall supply details upon request).

George O. Abell, Ph. D.
University of California,
Los Angeles

Los Angeles, CA 90024

Bennett Greenspan, M. D.
Wadsworth Veterans
Administration Hospital

Los Angeles, CA 90073

1. Rippman ET: The moon and the birth rate. Am J Obstet Gynecol 74:148-150, 1957
2. Menaker W, Menaker A: Lunar periodicity in human reproduction: a likely biological time. Am J Obstet Gynecol 77:905-914, 1959
3. Menaker W: Lunar periodicity with reference to live births. Am J Obstet Gynecol 98:1002-1004, 1967.
4. Osley M, Summerville D, Borst LB: Natality and the moon. Am J Obstet Gynecol 117:413-415, 1973.

The F test or F ratio. Some pages ago,[29] we introduced the concept of the standard error of the mean. But the mean is not unique in this characteristic. We have also a variation which occurs in deviations from the mean from sample to sample. A method of comparing samples to determine the ratio of their variances is known as Snedecor's *F test*,[30] or sometimes referred to as the *F ratio*.[31] Given two or more samples, if the variance of the samples were the same, the ratio would be equal to unity (1.00). But, in practice, we seldom find this perfect relationship and as the variances of the samples vary, the index of the variance departs from 1.00 in a greater, rather than lesser, degree. The ratio is represented by *F*. In practice, statisticians divide the square of the larger standard deviation of the one sample by the square of the smaller standard deviation of the other sample and then refer to a table of *F*.

The *F* test is frequently used to test generalizations concerning groups: the Hottentots are better drivers than the Patagonians. It is also used to test the variation *among* the groups versus the variation *between* the groups. The *F* test is a test of the homogeneity of variance. As the size of the *F* value increases, the probability of rejecting the null hypothesis increases.

Needless to say, we are dealing with somewhat sophisticated statistical concepts. The purpose here is not to have you understand these thoroughly but merely to provide enough insight so that when, in your reading of research, you come across such statistical tests and

[29] See p. 119 ff.
[30] G. W. Snedecor, *Statistical Methods.* Ames Iowa: Iowa State College Press, 1956.
[31] So named for Sir Ronald A. Fisher who introduced the idea and method in 1924.

techniques that you will have some appreciation of what the researcher is attempting to do to safeguard the integrity of his conclusion.

— —

Practical Application of the Preceding Discussion

Project 1. Earlier in these pages—at the close of chapter 3—you were directed to locate five research reports and to analyze them with marginal comments according to the example cited earlier in the chapter. Project 2 in that Practical Application Section indicated that you would be asked later to explain the statistical aspects of those reports.

Go back, now, to the reports which you analyzed earlier and, selecting the statistical parts of each report, explain what the author of the report was doing in presenting the statistical data. Obviously, you have been given merely a superficial introduction into statistical procedures in research, but as far as possible, comment upon the statistics and the use of them in making the report meaningful to the reader.

Should the reports that you chose for the project at the close of chapter 3 not contain any statistical concepts, select five other reports which have statistical implications and explain them.

— —

CHAPTER 7   Reading and Understanding Historical Research

The Problems of History
How Historical Researchers Solve Them

Historical research is essentially no different from any other kind of research. History, too, has its problems and its enigmas. And it is these that are the basis for historical research. In the events of the past unanswered questions still remain. We need look only at the many investigations, the much difference of opinion that has been occasioned by the assassination of John Fitzgerald Kennedy to authenticate this claim. Unresolved issues still hover over the records in the archives. It is with the problems of history and the meaning of history that historical research is concerned.

Earlier in this book we defined research generally as "a methodical quest in the search for truth and the solution of problems." Later, we said: "The prime function of research is to deal with problems; . . . and by problems we mean those tantalizing, enigmatical, unresolved roadblocks to knowledge and human progress for which there exists no answer whatsoever."[1] Certainly, in the long annals of history there exist many problems in need of resolution.

Questions abound for which we have no clear answer. Why did Longstreet hesitate three hours before ordering General Pickett to make the charge at Gettysburg? Why were the conditions on the English Channel suddenly ultra-propitious for the crossing of the allied forces? What happened at Dallas? Why was there an 18-minute blackout on the Watergate tapes? Questions, questions, questions—all unanswered or for which no conclusive and undisputed answer has been forthcoming. All are roadblocks to human knowledge. All, problems for historical research.

---

[1] See pp. 2–3.

Incidentally, you may find expressed in the literature some very provincial viewpoints. You may encounter the thought that historical research is not genuine research. Those who deny that historical research is a true genre of research methodology lack insight into the global concept of research methodology generally. Some schools of thought contend that unless research is "experimental" it lacks the qualifications for true research. Others exhibit quite equal fervor for so-called "statistical" research. They argue that unless all problems are formulated in terms of the null hypothesis and tested statistically that the project fails to qualify as genuine research. Other variant viewpoints concerning the nature of research are also expressed in the literature from time to time. Narrow parochialism has no place in modern research methodology. Research searches for the truth wherever that truth may lie.

No one methodology has a monopoly on the research process. The data alone govern the choice of the methodology which researchers must employ. Historical research has a methodological genre in its own right, dictated by the uniqueness of historical data and its primary function is to try to resolve the unanswered questions of history, to solve the problems of the past, or to discover what may be significant for the present from the facts of the past.

THE UNIQUENESS OF HISTORICAL DATA

Historical data is unique. They consist of written records, artifacts, recorded observations, letters and memoranda, photographs, entries in diaries, personal memorabilia, and conversations or comments recorded on magnetic tape. This is the documentary grist of historical research, and these contain the facts with which historical researchers must work.

But facts of any kind are elusive and unstable. This thesis we developed in chapter 5, and nowhere is the elusiveness of fact more pronounced that in historical research. "What we call facts is merely a way of identifying the trustworthy observations of the phenomena around us."[2] Merely to observe and to record is not enough. Those who write history must do so so that their record is credible: others must be able to trust what they have seen, believe what they have heard, and accept what they have recorded. There are tests for historical data quite as criterional as those applied to the null hypothesis.

Historical data is particularly elusive and subject to the human equation. Unless recorded on magnetic tape, preservation of the event depends upon its perception and its recording by a human being. This injects into the system all types of variables: the ability of the person recording to observe accurately and dispassionately what he sees, to express adequately in words what he is attempting to say, to be, in fact, a perfect reflecting surface from which the fact is transmitted without aberration or distortion. This is next to humanly impossible. And yet, the historical researcher must try to get as close to the actual historical event as possible. We can thus see the magnitude of the difficulty facing those who would engage in solving the problems of history.

A thin intervening veil of conditioning circumstances always separates the actual happening from the recorded fact no matter how faithful the recording. An event happens. Someone snaps a picture of it. The eyewitness has captured the event. That, you say, is a record of what actually occurred. But is it? What about the angle of the camera shot? Does it portray what another observer might have seen on the opposite side or at 90 degrees on either side of the photographer? Several people witness a single event. Quiz them carefully

---

[2] See p. 68.

and individually. You will probably come away with as many variant reports as there were individuals who saw the happening. On the night that Lincoln was shot, each person in Ford's Theater probably had his own version of what transpired. What *really* happened? And what are the lessons of history? What generalizations can we make from the events of the past? These are the questions, these are the problems with which the historical researcher wrestles.

Indigenous to historical fact is the presence of historical bias. Those who would read historical research and understand it need to understand all of its implications and shortcomings. They need to recognize its limitations as well as its possibilities. They need to insist on a precision of fact as rigorously as those who read research in any other area. Those who confidently affirm that Columbus discovered the New World on October 12, 1492 are guilty of historical misstatement. It was *not* Columbus, but one, Rodrigo de Triana, the lookout on the *Nina*, who in the light of a full tropical moon at two o'clock in the morning, shouted *Tierra! Tierra!* and actually "discovered" the New World in the island that Columbus later that day christened San Salvador.

Inconsequential, you say. Yes, but facts are facts and historical research demands as high a degree of precision from those who would engage in it as scientific or statistical research demands of its practitioners.

KINDS OF HISTORICAL FACT

Data for historical research are of two kinds: *primary data* and *secondary data*. We shall discuss each of these two types separately.

Primary data. Primary data are those data which lie closest to the source of the event. They afford the nearest proximity to the problem; and they give the researcher the best possible close-up view of what happened and why it happened. History, by its very nature, postulates a time barrier between the event and those who study the event—or, for that matter, those who record the event. This tends to dull the sharpness of the fact, as we have discussed in paragraphs preceding. But, for those who would solve the problems that history poses, it is mandatory that they get as clear and as close a view of the subject matter from which the problem springs. To do so is to utilize *primary data.* We may define primary data as *those data beyond which we cannot go in seeking the truth with respect to an historical event.* Those who actively participated in a movement, those who actually witnessed a happening, the words of a person who expressed his thoughts and feelings about his own participation in an event, and similar situations which take us with ultimate close-upness to the fact which we are investigating are all primary data.

I walk out of my home to get into my automobile. My attention is attracted by a whining noise, a series of muffled detonations, and a dark shadow around me. I look up. A plane, flames streaming from underside passes dangerously low, tangles with the high tension wires a quarter of a mile away, flips over, and disintegrates in an open field in a mass of flames. The pilot perishes in the crash. I am—as sole observer—closest to the happenings—the data—surrounding the crash. My facts regarding the accident are *primary* data.

I am a news reporter. I jump into my car, go down to the office, sit down at my typewriter and write an "eyewitness" account of the crash. The evening paper carries it as a front page feature. Thousands of readers read my words in the early evening edition.

A man reads my account coming home on the train. At dinner that evening he recounts what he has read to his wife, his son, and daughter. For them, it is no longer primary data.

Secondary data. Every stage of data transmission endangers the primary integrity of the data. Those who read my account in the evening edition cannot experience what I experienced when I saw the actual crash. Their words in recounting the incident will be different from mine. Even my words in the printed column may not reproduce the emotional overtones I experienced when witnessing the actual event. They who read my words also have varying degrees of reading skill. They comprehend my thoughts unevenly: some details they remember more vividly than others. In relating my thoughts they recast my words into their own vocabulary. The data are diluted. They are second-hand and largely suspect for purposes of research. The historical researcher, therefore, seeks only primary data in solving the problems of history. Those who read research should be careful to inspect the data for evidence of its primary quality.

The Great Fire of London took place in 1666. I read an account of the fire. Glancing down at a footnote, I notice that the author has gleaned his data from a history of London, published in New York, and dated 1927! I fear he has just destroyed my confidence in him as a competent researcher on the Great Fire. Perhaps he did not know that during the fire Samuel Pepys stood on the south bank and witnessed the great conflagration and left us an eyewitness account in his famous *Diary*. Had I seen Pepys instead of the unknown author of the 1927 volume in the footnote I may have had more credence in the study.

Some years ago I was doing a study on the language practices in the early American college.[3] I came across a statement in an early 20th century history of Harvard University that English was forbidden to be spoken within the precincts of the early college. The history was written by a distinguished historian and a graduate of Harvard University. I read the statement with interest, but at best—and especially for research purposes—the statement was mere hearsay. I could not admit it to my study without *primary* data to confirm it. If such a rule for the student body of Harvard College did exist then, I reasoned, it must have been written somewhere in the annals of the college at the time that it was enforced. If I could find that source, I would have uncovered the primary source upon which the distinguished historian's statement was based. The hunt was on.

After a Sherlock Holmes sleuthing through the early records of Harvard University, I found it. In a volume entitled, *Statua Harvardini* [The Statutes of Harvard] published in 1642, there were the words that I sought:

> *Scholares vernacula lingua intra Collegii limites nullo praetextu utantur, nisi ad orationem aut aliud aliquod exercitum publicum Anglice habendum evocati fuerint.*[4]

Those who read Latin may comprehend its meaning. They may compare the statement of the eminent historian who said that English was *entirely* forbidden within the precincts of Harvard College. Here was a source—the Latin statement of the prohibition printed in the regulations of the college six years after its founding—beyond which it was not possible to go. This was primary data.

---

[3]Paul D. Leedy, "A History of the Origin and Development of Instruction in Reading Improvement at the College Level," Unpublished dissertation, New York University, 1958.

[4]*Statua Harvardini*, 13 (1642) issued in facsimile by the University in the *College Book*, I, 45.

THE QUESTION OF EVIDENCE: INTERNAL AND EXTERNAL

There is still another consideration that must claim the attention of the historical researcher and, consequently, those who would read and understand historical research. That is the matter of *evidence* or, as some authorities call it, *criticism*.

You have probably been aware that throughout the text whenever we have discussed the research process, we have been on the alert for those insidious factors which may jeopardize the integrity of the research quality. Bias is an infectious contamination that may creep unnoticed into the most carefully designed research projects. Failure to provide adequate control in experimental studies, statistical misuse of measures, and the drawing of unwarranted conclusions from merely segments of the data all constitute imperfections in the research design. These are hazards against which the researcher and the reader of research must always be on the alert to recognize.

In addition to the matters that we have previously mentioned in these pages, with historical research we have the additional matter of *evidence*. Evidence is of two kinds: *external* and *internal*. We shall discuss each briefly.

External evidence. External evidence asks of the data—usually the document, but it may be the artifact or any other type of data—one question: "Is it genuine?" In fact, the first question that a historian must decide about a document is whether it is genuine or a counterfeit. Fakes are not uncommon. We are all familiar with instances of paintings which have hung in art galleries and museums for years and have been admired by thousands only to have turned out not to be Vermeers, or Rembrandts, or Murillos—but fakes. The literary world has also learned to its chagrin that it is not without counterfeits. Consider Thomas Chatterton who passed off the famous "Rowley Manuscripts" on an unsuspecting seventeenth century as the work of a 15th century priest of Bristol called Thomas Rowley (a purely fictitious character).

For years, textbooks in anthropology taught of the existence of Piltdown Man, and *Eoanthropus Dawsoni* was accepted by most pre-historians, archeologists, and anthropologists as a scientific fact. It was a carefully planned hoax that fooled most experts.

The question: "Is it real? Is it genuine?" is by no means merely academic, it is far from being pointless. Literary history and the world of objects of art have had their ample share of forgeries.

Internal evidence. Internal evidence considers quite another question. It asks, not "Is it genuine?" but, rather, "What does it mean?" What did the author mean when he wrote these words; or the speaker, when he uttered them; or, of the artifact, what was its purpose and use? This type of evidence, or criticism, gets at the intention *behind* the word. On November 17, 1863, President Lincoln spoke at the dedication of the Union Cemetery at Gettysburg. In his concluding sentence he said: . . . "that that government of the *people*, by the *people*, for the *people* should not perish from the earth." Those who heard Mr. Lincoln that day recall how he gave a decided emphasis to the word *people*. What idea was Mr. Lincoln trying to convey? What was he attempting to say to the crowd on Cemetery Ridge in Gettysburg? The historian of that event would have to grapple with that fact of emphasis. Internal evidence asks, "What does it mean? What do the words purport to convey?"

Those who read research should be sensitive to the attempt of the historical researcher to deal with internal evidence and should consider how logical and reasoned a conclusion is formulated by the researcher in the face of the words with which he has to deal.

WHAT DOES HISTORY ITSELF MEAN?

Perhaps an enlargement of the concept of internal evidence is the problem that faces the historical researcher in gathering meaning from the events of the past. What can the present learn from the record of the past? That is a general problem. That is an important consideration for those who seek light from the annals of history on the perplexing problems of today. Perhaps this can be best shown by closing this section of the chapter with a chapter from one of the world's greatest modern historians, Arnold Toynbee. His problem was this: If we look at the great empires, not as outsiders, but through the eyes of their own citizens, what do we discover? When we compare this "inside" view with an "outside" and centuries-later view, what then do we discover? Here is Toynbee's "research report" that answers those questions. Notice also how interesting, yet factual, the writing of historical research can be.

The Mirage of Immortality

Arnold J. Toynbee

This Column for Your Comments on the Study*

If we look at these universal states, not as alien observers but through the eyes of their own citizens, we shall find that these not only desire that these earthly commonwealths of theirs should live forever but actually believe that the immortality of these human institutions is assured, and this sometimes in the teeth of contemporary events which, to an observer posted at a different standpoint in time or space, declare beyond question that this particular universal state is at that very moment in its last agonies. Why is it, such an observer might well ask, that, in defiance of apparently plain facts, the citizens of a universal state are prone to regard it, not as a night's shelter in the wilderness, but as the Promised Land, the goal of human endeavors? It should be said, however, that this sentiment is confined to the citizens of universal states established by indigenous empire-builders. No Indian, for example, either desired or foretold the immortality of the British Rāj.

In the history of the Roman Empire, which was the universal state of the Hellenic civilization, we find the generation that had witnessed the establishment of the *Pax Augusta* asserting, in evidently sincere good faith, that the Empire and the City that had built it have been endowed with a common immortality. Tibullus (*circa* 54-18 B.C.) sings of "the walls of the eternal city" while Virgil (70-19 B.C.) makes his Iuppiter, speaking of the future Roman scions of Aeneas' race, say: "I give them empire without end." Livy writes with the same assurance of "the city founded for eternity." Horace, sceptic though he was, in claiming immortality for his Odes, takes as his concrete measure of eternity the repetition

*In this column, (1) indicate the statement of the historical research problem, (2) the facts which are presented to support—or resolve—the problem, and (3) the conclusion which is reached in resolving the problem. Add any other observations which will reflect your insight into the research process or the contents of this chapter.

Arnold J. Toynbee, *A Study of History*, abridged ed., Oxford University Press, New York, 1957, vol. II, pp. 4-6, 8-10. Reprinted by permission.

of the annual round of the religious ritual of the Roman city state. The Odes are still alive on the lips of men. How much longer their "immortality" will continue is uncertain, for the number of those who can quote them has been sadly diminished in recent times by changes in educational fashions; but at least they have lived four or five times as long as the Roman pagan ritual. More than four hundred years after the age of Horace and Virgil, after the sack of Rome by Alaric has already announced the end, we find the Gallic poet Rutilius Namatianus still defiantly asserting Rome's immortality and Saint Jerome, in scholarly retreat at Jerusalem, interrupting his theological labours to express his grief and stupefaction in language almost identical with that of Rutilius. The pagan official and the Christian Father are united in their emotional reactions to an event which, as we now see it, had been inevitable for generations.

The shock administered by the fall of Rome in A.D. 410 to the citizens of a transient universal state which they had mistaken for an everlasting habitation has its counterpart in the shock suffered by the subjects of the Arab Caliphate when Baghdad fell to the Mongols in A.D. 1258. In the Roman world the shock was felt from Palestine to Gaul; in the Arab world from Farghānah to Andalusia. The intensity of the psychological effect is even more remarkable in this than in the Roman case; for, by the time when Hūlāgū gave the 'Abbasid Caliphate its *coup de grâce*, its sovereignty had been ineffective for three or four centuries over the greater part of the vast domain nominally subject to it. This halo of an illusory immortality, worn by moribund universal states, often persuades the more prudent barbarian leaders, in the very act of parcelling out their dominions among themselves, to acknowledge an equally illusory subjection. The Amalung leaders of the Arian Ostrogoths and the Buwayhid leaders of the Shi'i Daylamis sought title for their conquests by ruling them, in official theory, as viceregents of the Emperor at Constantinople and the Caliph at Baghdad respectively; and, though this tactful handling of a senile universal state did not avail, in their case, to avert the doom to which both these warbands condemned themselves by clinging to their distinctive religious heresies, the same political manoeuvre was brilliantly successful when executed by fellow barbarians who had the sagacity or good fortune to be at the same time impeccable in their professions of religious faith. Clovis the Frank, for example, the most successful of all the founders of barbarian successor-states of the Roman Empire, followed up his conversion to Catholicism by obtaining from the Emperor Anastasius in distant Constantinople the title of proconsul with consular insignia. His success is attested by the fact that in later ages no less than eighteen royal Louis, reigning in the land that he conquered, bore a modified variant of his name.

Comments on the Study

The Ottoman Empire, which became the universal state of a Byzantine civilization, exhibited the same characteristics of illusory immortality at a time when it had already become "the Sick Man of Europe." The ambitious warlords who were carving out for themselves successor-states—a Mehmed 'Ali in Egypt and Syria, an 'Ali of Yannina in Albania and Greece, and a Pasvanoghlu of Viddin in the north-western corner of Rumelia—were sedulous in doing in the Padishah's name all that they were doing to his detriment in their own private interests. When the Western Powers followed in their footsteps, they adopted the same fictions. Great Britain, for example, administered Cyprus from 1878 and Egypt from 1882 in the name of the Sultan at Constantinople until she found herself at war with Turkey in 1914.

The Mughal universal state of the Hindu civilization displays the same features. Within half a century of the Emperor Awrangzib's death in A.D. 1707, an empire which had once exercised effective sovereignty over the greater part of the Indian subcontinent had been whittled down to a torso some 250 miles long and 100 miles broad. After another half-century it had been reduced to the circuit of the walls of the Red Fort at Delhi. Yet, 150 years after A.D. 1707, a descendant of Akbar and Awrangzib was still squatting on their throne, and might have been left there much longer if the Mutineers of 1857 had not forced this poor puppet, against his wishes, to give his blessing to their revolt against a raj from overseas which had, after a period of anarchy, replaced the long-extinct Mughal Rāj which he still symbolized.

A still more remarkable testimony to the tenacity of the belief in the immortality of universal states is the practice of evoking their ghosts after they have proved themselves mortal by expiring. The 'Abbasid Caliphate of Baghdad was thus resuscitated in the shape of the 'Abbasid Caliphate of Cairo, and the Roman Empire in the shape of the Holy Roman Empire of the West and the East Roman Empire of Orthodox Christendom; and the empire of the Ts'in and Han dynasties in the shape of the Sui and T'ang Empire of the Far Eastern civilization. The surname of the founder of the Roman Empire was revived in the titles Kaiser and Czar, and the title of Caliph, which originally meant successor of Muhammad, after haunting Cairo, passed on to Istanbul, where it survived until its abolition at the hands of Westernizing revolutionists in the twentieth century.

These are only a selection from the wealth of historical examples illustrating the fact that the belief in the immortality of universal states survives for centuries after it has been confuted by plain hard facts. What are the causes of this strange phenomenon?

One manifest cause is the potency of the impression made by the founders and the great rulers of universal states, an impression handed on to a receptive posterity with an emphasis which exaggerates an imposing truth into an overwhelming legend. Another cause is the impressiveness of the institution itself, apart from the genius displayed by its greatest rulers.

And yet the reality of these universal states was something very different from the brilliant surface that they presented to Aelius Aristeides and their other panegyrists in various ages and various climes.

An obscure divinity of the Nubian marches of the Egyptiac universal state was transfigured by the genius of Hellenic mythology into a mortal king of the Ethiopians who had the misfortune to be loved by Eos, the immortal Goddess of the Dawn. The goddess besought her fellow Olympians to confer on her human lover the immortality which she and her peers enjoyed; and, jealous though they were of their divine privileges, she teased them into yielding at last to her feminine importunity. Yet even this grudging gift was marred by a fatal flaw; for the eager goddess had forgotten that the Olympians' immortality was mated with an everlasting youth, and the other immortals had spitefully taken care to grant her no more than her bare request. The consequence was both ironic and tragic. After a honeymoon that flashed past in the twinkling of an Olympian eye, Eos and her now immortal but still inexorably ageing mate found themselves condemned for eternity to grieve together over Tithonus's hapless plight. A senility to which the merciful hand of death could never set a term was an affliction that no mortal man could ever be made to suffer, and an eternal grief was an obsession that left no room for any other thought or feeling.

For any human soul or human institution an immortality in This World would prove a martyrdom, even if it were unaccompanied by either physical decrepitude or mental senility. "In this sense," wrote the philosophic Emperor Marcus Aurelius (A.D. 161–180), "it would be true to say that any man of forty who is endowed with moderate intelligence has seen—in the light of the uniformity of Nature—the entire Past and Future"; and, if this estimate of the capacity of human souls for experience strikes the reader as an inordinately low one, he may find the reason in the age in which Marcus lived; for an "Indian Summer" is an age of boredom. The price of the Roman Peace was the forfeiture of Hellenic liberty; and, though that liberty might always have been the privilege of a minority, and this privileged minority might have turned irresponsible and oppressive, it was manifest in retrospect that the turbulent wickedness of the Ciceronian climax of an Hellenic "Time of Troubles" had provided a wealth of exciting and inspiring themes for Roman public speakers which their epigoni in a smugly ordered Trajanic epoch might conventionally condemn as horrors, not *nostri saeculi*, but must secretely envy as they found themselves perpetually failing in their laborious efforts to substitute far-fetched artifice for the stimulus of importunate life.

On the morrow of the breakdown of the Hellenic society Plato,

Comments on the Study

anxiously seeking to safeguard it against a further fall by pegging it in a securely rigid posture, had idealized the comparative stability of the Egyptiac culture; and a thousand years later, when this Egyptiac culture was still in being while the Hellenic civilization had arrived at its last agonies, the last of the Neo-platonists pushed their reputed master's sentiment to an almost frenzied pitch of uncritical admiration.

Thanks to the obstinacy of the Egyptiac universal state in again and again insisting on returning to life after its body had been duly laid on the salutary funeral pyre, the Egyptiac civilization lived to see its contemporaries—the Minoan, the Sumeric, and the Indus culture—all pass away and give place to successors of a younger generation, some of which had passed away in their turn while the Egyptiac society still kept alive. Egyptiac students of history could have observed the birth and death of the First Syriac, Hittite, and Babylonic offspring of the Sumeric civilization and the rise and decline of the Syriac and Hellenic offspring of the Minoan. Yet the fabulously long-drawn-out epilogue to the broken-down Egyptiac society's natural term of life was but an alternation of long stretches of boredom with hectic bouts of demonic energy, into which this somnolent society was galvanized by the impact of alien bodies social.

The same rhythm of trance-like somnolence alternating with outbursts of fanatical xenophobia can be discerned in the epilogue to the history of the Far Eastern civilization in China. The tincture of Far Eastern Christian culture in the Mongols who had forced upon China an alien universal state evoked a reaction in which the Mongols were evicted and their dominion replaced by the indigenous universal state of the Ming. Even the Manchu barbarians, who stepped into the political vacuum created by the Ming's collapse, and whose taint of Far Eastern Christian culture was less noticeable than their receptivity in adopting the Chinese way of life, aroused a popular opposition which, in Southern China at any rate, never ceased to maintain itself underground and broke out into the open again in the T'aip'ing insurrection of A.D. 1852-64. The infiltration of the Early Modern Western civilization, in its Catholic Christian form in the sixteenth and seventeenth centuries provoked the proscription of Catholicism in the first quarter of the eighteenth century. The blasting open of the seagates of China for Western trade between A.D. 1839 and A.D. 1861 provoked the retort of the anti-Western "Boxer" rising of A.D. 1900; and the Manchu Dynasty was overthrown in A.D. 1911 in retribution for the double crime of being ineradicably alien itself and at the same time showing itself incompetent to keep the now far more formidable alien force of Western penetration at bay.

Happily life is kinder than legend, and the sentence of immortality which mythology passed on Tithonus is commuted, for the benefit of the universal states of history, to a not interminable

136

longevity. Marcus's disillusioned man of forty must die at last though he may outlive his zest for life by fifty or sixty years, and a universal state that kicks again and again against the pricks of death will weather away in the course of ages, like the pillar of salt that was fabled to be the petrified substance of a once living woman.

Comments on the Study

— —

Practical Application of the Preceding Discussion

At this point, you should be able to read research with a degree of maturity and understanding that you may have lacked when you began the study of this book. For that reason, you will be asked to evaluate and to discuss with a rationale for your comments the research reports that follow. To assist you in this, you will find below a research report critique form which may guide you in considering those factors which are most important in reading and understanding any research report.

Below, you will find a Critical Evaluation Form for the Reading of Research Reports. It gathers up all of the significant items discussed in this text with respect to reading research reports. It can also be used to give you a percentage index of the degree to which any research report meets the criteria discussed in these pages. Use it in reading and evaluating the reports on page 139 and following.

A Critical Evaluation Form for
The Reading of Research Reports

Use the following questions as a checklist. It will help you to evaluate published research and will serve as a review of the principal items discussed in this book.

	Yes	No
Is It Research?		
1. Is the problem clearly stated?	——	——
2. Is the problem suggested in the title of the report?	——	——
3. Is the research testing or positing any hypotheses?	——	——
4. Does the research report refer to the efforts of other researchers?	——	——
5. Are the data set forth clearly?	——	——
6. Does the research report set forth any conclusions as a result of the analysis of the data?	——	——
The Format of the Report		
7. Is the research report a clear exposition of what the researcher has done?	——	——

8. *Is the title of the report explicit and communicative?* ____ ____

9. *Does the report have an abstract or summary?* ____ ____

10. *Is the problem immediately apparent either through the title or so placed in the report that it is easily found?* ____ ____

11. *Is the report supported by documentation?* ____ ____

Research Methodology

12. *Has the author of the report identified the research methodology, or is it apparent on the face of the report?* ____ ____

13. *Have the data been presented in summary form through the media of graphs, charts, tables or other means of factual summary?* ____ ____

14. *Are the data in the graphs, tables, etc. interpreted and explained in the report?* ____ ____

15. *Are the captions and identification of the sections of the report clearly indicated? Is the presentation easily read?* ____ ____

16. *Are the data from primary sources?* ____ ____

17. *Do you discern any attempt to avoid bias on the part of the researcher or in the design of the research?* ____ ____

18. *Has the author of the report identified and acknowledged the possibility of bias?* ____ ____

19. *Is the methodology clearly explained, especially the statistical methodology?* ____ ____

20. *Are the data subjected to a logical statistical treatment and has the researcher given the rationale for the particular statistics used?* ____ ____

21. *If the null hypothesis is being tested, does the researcher indicate whether the hypothesis has been accepted or rejected?* ____ ____

22. *Does the researcher indicate how the sample was chosen or how randomicity was safeguarded?* ____ ____

23. *Even though the statistics may be somewhat more sophisticated than you are able to understand, can you follow the statistical rationale?* ____ ____

24. *Do the data presented warrant the conclusions the researcher draws?* ____ ____

25. *Would you rate this a satisfactory attempt at reporting research?* ____ ____

To evaluate the report according to this form, do the following:

1. *Add up all checkmarks in the "Yes" column, and do likewise for the "No" column. Enter the totals here* ____ ____

 X4 *X4*

2. *Multiple each total by 4* ____ ____

3. *Put the figure resulting from the multiplying the "Yes"*
   column by 4 in this box.
It is the percentage of positive qualities in the report.

FURTHER STUDIES FOR READING AND ANALYSIS

Reference Groups, Membership Groups, and Attitude Change*

Alberta Engvall Siegel and Sidney Siegel

In social psychological theory, it has long been recognized that an individual's *membership groups* have an important influence on the values and attitudes he holds. More recently, attention has also been given to the influence of his *reference groups*, the groups in which he aspires to attain or maintain membership. In a given area, membership groups and reference groups may or may not be identical. They are identical when the person aspires to *maintain* membership in the group of which he is a part; they are disparate when the group in which the individual aspires to *attain* membership is one in which he is not a member. It has been widely asserted that both membership and reference groups affect the attitudes held by the individual.[1]

The present study is an examination of the attitude changes which occur over time when reference groups and membership groups are identical and when they are disparate. The study takes advantage of a field experiment which occurred in the social context of the lives of the subjects, concerning events considered vital by them. The subjects were not aware that their membership and reference groups were of research interest; in fact, they did not know that the relevant information about these was available to the investigators.

The field experiment permitted a test of the general hypothesis that both the amount and the direction of a person's attitude change over time depends on the attitude norms of his membership group (whether or not that group is chosen by him) and on the attitude norms of his reference group.

This hypothesis is tested with subjects who shared a common reference group at the time of the initial assessment of attitudes. They were then randomly assigned to alternative membership groups, some being assigned to the chosen group and others to a

This Column for Your Comments on the Report*

*In a sense, your comments in this column are a kind of final examination of your ability to read a research report appreciatively and understandably. Demonstrate your ability to read research by reflecting through your comments your comprehension of the subject matter in this text.

---

[1] M. Sherif and C. Sherif, *Groups in Harmony and Tension* (New York: Harper & Row, Publishers, 1953).

*From the *Journal of Abnormal and Social Psychology*, 1957, *55*, pp. 360–364. Used by permission of the authors and publisher. This study was supported by grants from the Committee for the Study of American Values at Stanford University and from the Stanford Value Theory Project.

nonchosen group. Attitudes were reassessed after a year of experience in these alternative membership groups with divergent attitude norms. During the course of the year, some subjects came to take the imposed (initially nonpreferred) membership group as their reference group. Attitude change after the year was examined in terms of the membership group and reference group identifications of the subjects at that time.

THE FIELD EXPERIMENT

The *Ss** of this study were women students at a large private coeducational university. The study was initiated shortly before the end of their freshman year, when they all lived in the same large freshman dormitory to which they had been assigned upon entering the university. At this university, all women move to new housing for their sophomore year. Several types of housing are available to them: a large dormitory, a medium-sized dormitory, several small houses which share common dining facilities, and a number of former sorority houses which have been operated by the university since sororities were banished from the campus. These latter are located among the fraternity houses on Fraternity Row, and are therefore known as "Row houses." Although the Row houses are lower in physical comfort than most of the other residences for women, students consider them higher in social status. This observation was confirmed by a poll of students,[2] in which over 90 per cent of the respondents stated that Row houses for women were higher in social status than non-Row houses, the remaining few disclaiming any information concerning status differences among women's residences.

In the Spring of each year, a "drawing" is held for housing for the subsequent year. All freshmen must participate in this drawing, and any other student who wishes to change her residence may participate. It is conducted by the office of the Dean of Women, in cooperation with woman student leaders. Any participant's ballot is understood to be secret. The woman uses the ballot to rank the houses in the order of her preference. After submitting this ballot, she draws a number from the hopper. The rank of that number determines the likelihood that her preference will be satisfied.

In research reported earlier,[3] a random sample was drawn from the population of freshman women at this university, several

---

[2] S. Siegel, "Certain Determinants and Correlates of Authoritarianism," *Genetic Psychology Monographs*, 1954, *49*, pp. 187-299.

[3] S. Siegel, *op. cit.*

*Ss means "Subjects."

tests were administered to the Ss in that sample, and (unknown to the Ss) their housing preferences for the forthcoming sophomore year were observed by the investigator. The Ss were characterized as "high status oriented" if they listed a Row house as their first choice, and were characterized as "low status oriented" if they listed a non-Row house as their first choice. The hypothesis under test, drawn from reference group theory and from theoretical formulations concerning authoritarianism, was that high status orientation is a correlate of authoritarianism. The hypothesis was confirmed: freshman women who listed a Row house as their first choice for residence scored significantly higher on the average in authoritarianism, as measured by the E-F scale,[4] than did women who listed a non-Row house as their first choice. The present study is a continuation of the one described, and uses as its Ss only those members of the original sample who were "high status oriented," i.e., preferred to live in a Row house for the sophomore year. In the initial study, of the 95 Ss whose housing choices were listed, 39 were "high status oriented," i.e., demonstrated that the Row was their reference group by giving a Row house as their first choice in the drawing. Of this group, 28 were available to serve as Ss for the follow-up or "change" study which is the topic of the present paper. These women form a homogeneous subsample in that at the conclusion of their freshman year they shared a common membership group (the freshman dormitory) and a common reference group (the Row). These Ss, however, had divergent experiences during their sophomore year; nine were Row residents during that year (having drawn sufficiently small numbers in the housing drawing to enable them to be assigned to the group of their choice) and the other 19 lived in non-Row houses during that year (having drawn numbers too large to enable them to be assigned to the group of their choice).

E-F scores were obtained from each of the 28 Ss in the course of a large-scale testing program administered to most of the women students at the university. Anonymity was guaranteed to the Ss, but a coding procedure permitted the investigators to identify each respondent and thereby to isolate the Ss and compare each S's second E-F score with her first.

To prevent the Ss from knowing that they were participating in a follow-up study, several procedures were utilized: *(a)* many persons who had not served in the earlier study were included in the second sample, *(b)* the testing was introduced as being part of a nation-wide study to establish norms, *(c)* the test administra-

Comments on the Report

---

[4]T. Adorno, *et al.*, *The Authoritarian Personality* (New York: Harper & Row, Publishers, 1950); H. G. Gough, "Studies of Social Intolerance: I, Some Psychological and Sociological Correlates of Anti-Semitism," *Journal of Social Psychology*, 1951, *33*, pp. 237–246.

tors were different persons from those who had administered the initial tests, *(d)* *S*s who informed the test administrator that they had already taken the "Public Opinion Questionnaire" (E-F scale) were casually told that this did not disqualify them from participating in the current study.

The *S*s had no hint that the research was in any way related to their housing arrangements. Testing was conducted in classrooms as well as in residences, and all procedures and instructions were specifically designed to avoid any arousal of the salience of the housing groups in the frame of reference of the research.

The annual housing drawing was conducted three weeks after the sophomore-year testing, and, as usual, each women's housing ballot was understood to be secret. In this drawing, each *S* had the opportunity to change her membership group, although a residence move is not required at the end of the sophomore year as it is at the end of the freshman year. If an S participated in this drawing, the house which she listed as her first choice on the ballot was identified by the investigators as her reference group. If she did not, it was evident that the house in which she was currently a member was the one in which she chose to continue to live, i.e., was her reference group. With the information on each *S*'s residence choice at the end of her freshman year, her assigned residence for her sophomore year, and her residence choice at the end of her sophomore year, it was possible to classify the subjects in three categories:

A. Women (*n* = 9) who had gained assignment to live on the Row during their sophomore year and who did not attempt to draw out of the Row at the end of that year;

B. Women (*n* = 11) who had not gained assignment to a Row house for the sophomore year and who drew for a Row house again after living in a non-Row house during the sophomore year; and

C. Women (*n* = 8) who had not gained assignment to a Row house for the sophomore year, and who chose to remain in a non-Row house after living in one during the sophomore year.

For all three groups of *S*s, as we have pointed out, membership group (freshman dormitory) and reference group (Row house) were common at the end of the freshman year. For Group A, membership and reference groups were disparate throughout the sophomore year. For Group B, membership and reference groups were disparate throughout the sophomore year. For Group C, membership and reference groups were initially disparate during the sophomore year but became identical because of a change in reference groups.

As will be demonstrated, the Row and the non-Row social groups differ in attitude norms, with Row residents being generally more authoritarian than non-Row residents. From social psychological theory concerning the influence of group norms on individuals' attitudes, it would be predicted that the different group identifications during the sophomore year of the three groups of *S*s would result in differential attitude change. Those who gained admittance to a Row house for the sophomore year (Group A) would be expected to show the least change in authoritarianism, for they spent that year in a social context which reinforced their initial attitudes. Group C *S*s would be expected to show the greatest change in authoritarianism, a change associated not only with their membership in a group (the non-Row group) which is typically low in authoritarianism, but also with their shift in reference groups, from Row to non-Row, i.e., from a group normatively higher in authoritarianism to a group normatively lower. The extent of attitude change in the *S*s in Group B would be expected to be intermediate, due to the conflicting influences of the imposed membership group (non-Row) and of the unchanged reference group (Row). The research hypothesis, then, is that between the time of the freshman-year testing and the sophomore-year testing, the extent of change in authoritarianism will be least in Group A, greater in Group B, and greatest in Group C. That is, in extent of attitude change, Group A < Group B < Group C.

RESULTS

Group norms. From the data collected in the large-scale testing program, it was possible to determine the group norms for authoritarian attitudes among the Row and the non-Row women at the university. The E-F scale was administered to all available Row residents (n = 303) and to a random sample of residents of non-Row houses (n = 101). These *S*s were sophomores, juniors, and seniors. The mean E-F score of the Row women was 90, while the mean E-F score of the non-Row was 81. The E-F scores of the two groups were demonstrated to differ at the $p<.001$ level (x^2 = 11.1) by the median test,[5] a nonparametric test, the data for which are shown in the table on page 144.

Attitude change. The central hypothesis of this study is that attitude change will occur differentially in Groups A, B, and C, and that it will occur in the direction which would be predicted

---

[5] S. Siegel, *Nonparametric Statistics: For the Behavioral Sciences* (New York: McGraw-Hill Book Co., Inc., 1956).

**Frequencies of E-F Scores Above and Below
Common Median for Row and Non-Row Residents**

	Residents of Non-Row Houses	Residents of Row Houses	Total
Above Median	36	166	202
Below Median	65	137	202
Total	101	303	404

from knowledge of the group norms among Row and non-Row residents in general. The 28 *S*s of this study had a mean E-F score of 102 at the end of their freshman year. The data reported above concerning authoritarianism norms for all women residing on campus would lead to the prediction that in general the *S*s would show a reduction in authoritarianism during the sophomore year but that this reduction would be differential in the three groups; from the knowledge that Row residents generally are higher in authoritarianism than non-Row residents, the prediction based on social group theory would be that Group A would show the smallest reduction in authoritarianism scores, Group B would show a larger reduction, and Group C would show the largest reduction. The data which permit a test of this hypothesis are given in Table 7-13. The Jonckheere test,[6] a nonparametric *k*-sample test which tests the null hypothesis that the three groups are from the same population against the alternative hypothesis that they are from different populations which are ordered in a specific way, was used with these data. By that test, the hypothesis is confirmed at the $p < .025$ level.

DISCUSSION

Substantively, the present study provides experimental verification of certain assertions in social group theory, demonstrating that attitude change over time is related to the group identification of the person—both his membership group identification and his reference group identification. The hypothesis that extent of attitude change would be different in the three subgroups of *S*s, depending on their respective membership group and reference group identifications, is confirmed at the $p < .025$ level; in extent of change in authoritarianism, Group A < Group B < Group C, as predicted.

---

[6] A. R. Jonckheere, "A Distribution-Free, k-Sample Test Against Ordered Alternatives," *Biometrika*, 1954, *41*, pp. 133–145.

Another way of looking at the data may serve to highlight the influence of membership groups and reference groups. At the end of the freshman year, the *S*s in Groups A, B, and C shared the same membership group and the same reference group. During the sophomore year, the *S*s in Group A shared one membership group while those in Groups B and C together shared another. From membership group theory, it would be predicted that the extent

Comments on the Report

Table 7-13. Freshman-Year and Sophomore-Year
E-F Scores of Subjects

| Group | E-F Score | | Difference |
	End of Freshman Year	End of Sophomore Year	
A	108	125	-17
	70	78	-8
	106	107	-1
	92	92	0
	80	78	2
	104	102	2
	143	138	5
	110	92	18
	114	80	34
B	76	117	-41
	105	107	-2
	88	82	6
	109	97	12
	98	83	15
	112	94	18
	101	82	19
	114	93	21
	104	81	23
	116	91	25
	101	74	27
C	121	126	-5
	87	79	8
	105	95	10
	97	81	16
	96	78	18
	108	73	35
	114	77	37
	88	49	39

of attitude change would be greater among the latter *S*s. This hypothesis is supported by the data (in Table 7-13); by the Mann-Whitney test,[7] the change scores of these two sets of *S*s (Group A

---

[7] S. Siegel, *Nonparametric Statistics, op. cit.,* pp. 116–127.

versus Groups B and C together) differ in the predicted direction at the $p<.025$ level. This finding illustrates the influence of *membership* groups on attitude change. On the other hand, at the conclusion of the sophomore year, the *S*s in Groups A and B shared a common reference group while those in Group C has come to share another. From reference group theory, it would be predicted that attitude change would be more extensive among the subjects who had changed reference groups (Group C) than among those who had not. This hypothesis is also supported by the data (in Table 7-13); by the Mann-Whitney test, the change scores of these two sets of Ss (Groups A and B together versus Group C) differ in the predicted direction at the $p<.05$ level. This finding illustrates the influence of *reference* groups on attitude change. Any inference from this mode of analysis (as contrasted with the main analysis of the data, by the Jonckheere test) must be qualified because of the nonindependence of the data on which the two Mann-Whitney tests are made, but it is mentioned here to clarify the role which membership and reference groups play in influencing attitude change.

The findings may also contribute to our understanding of processes affecting attitude change. The imposition of a membership group does have some effect on an individual's attitudes, even when the imposed group is not accepted by the individual as his reference group. This relationship is shown in the case of Group B. If the person comes to accept the imposed group as his reference group, as was the case with the Ss in Group C, then the change in his attitudes toward the level of the group norm is even more pronounced.

Methodologically, the study has certain features which may deserve brief mention. First, the study demonstrates that it is possible operationally to define the concept of reference group. The act of voting by secret ballot for the group in which one would like to live constitutes clear behavioral specification of one's reference group, and it is an act whose conceptual meaning can be so directly inferred that there is no problem of reliability of judgment in its categorization by the investigator. Second, the study demonstrates that a field study can be conducted which contains the critical feature of an experiment that is usually lacking in naturalistic situations: randomization. The determination of whether or not a woman student would be assigned to the living group of her choice was based on a random event: the size of the number she drew from the hopper. This fact satisfied the requirement that the treatment condition be randomized, and permitted sharper inferences than can usually be drawn from field studies. Third, the test behavior on which the conclusions of this study were based occurred in a context in which the salience of membership and reference groups was *not* aroused and in which no external sanctions from the relevant groups were operative. This feature of the design permitted the interpretation that the E-F scores represented the Ss' internalized attitudes.[8] Finally, the use of a paper-and-pencil measure of attitude and thus of attitude change, rather than the use of some more behavioral measure, is a deficiency of the present study. Moreover, the measure which was used suffers from a well-known circularity, based on the occurrence of pseudo-low scores.[9]

Comments on the Report

SUMMARY

In the social context of the lives of the subjects, and in a natural social experiment which provided randomization of the relevant condition effects, the influence of both membership and reference groups on attitude change was assessed. All subjects shared a common reference group at the start of the period of the study. When divergent membership groups with disparate attitude norms were socially imposed on the basis of a random event, attitude change in the subjects over time was a function of the normative attitudes of both imposed membership groups and the individuals' reference groups. The greatest attitude change occurred in subjects who came to take the imposed, initially nonpreferred, membership group as their reference group.

How Self-Perceived Knowledge, Actual Knowledge and Interest in Drugs Are Related

This Column for Your Comments on the Report*

Nicholas Galli, PH.D.
Associate Professor
Lehman College
City University of New York

ABSTRACT

The purpose of this study was to assess the relationship among student perception of knowledge, their levels of interest, and actual knowledge about drugs. Two-hundred and fifty-three college students responded to a knowledge and interest inventory as well as a knowledge test. Level of significance was set at .05 for both analysis of variance and correlation coefficients. No significant relationship was found to exist between perception of knowledge

---

[8] Sherif and Sherif, *op. cit.*, p. 218.
[9] Adorno, *op. cit.*, p. 771; S. Siegel, "Certain Determinants . . ." *op. cit.*, pp. 221–222.

Journal of Drug Education, Vol. 8(3), 1978, 197–202. © 1978, Baywood Publishing Co., Inc. Reprinted by permission.

*See footnote to this column p. 139.

and actual level of knowledge. A significant relationship existed between interest and perception of knowledge. It is evident from these findings that instructors must be wary of setting classroom objectives based solely upon student expressed knowledge as it is not always accurately reflected.

Comments on the Report

INTRODUCTION

Drug educators, like educators in all fields, are concerned with meeting the needs and interests of their students. They thus try to insure relevance in their curricula. Nowhere is this more important than in drug education where the goal goes beyond cognitive learning in an attempt to positively influence behavior.

Before teachers can establish objectives toward which to direct classroom instruction, they must determine student interests as well as their current level of knowledge. Do students perceive their level of knowledge accurately? While level of interest is subjective, objective criteria exist to assess the accuracy of student perception of their level of knowledge. If there is no significant relationship between a student's perception of his knowledge and his actual knowledge then the possibility of two types of errors exist. Firstly, if students see themselves as being less knowledgeable than they really are, time and effort will be spent by the teacher on projects of little worth. Students may also see themselves as being knowledgeable about topics they know little about. This creates the possibility of the instructor's avoiding discussion on needed topic areas. Accurate perception of cognitive information can be an invaluable aid to the instructor since it will help circumvent both types of errors.

Most studies in the area of perception have focused on students' perception of academic achievement. Self-perception of ability has been associated with college grades and other types of academic achievement [1-3]. These perceptions of academic achievement are fairly accurate since they are based on "a combination of factual and phenomenological factors." [4] A variety of concrete factors exist to aid the student in crystallizing his perceptions of personal achievement, including many years in a formal academic setting. Few such variables exist to aid his perceptions within specific cognitive areas. Those that do are more nebulous and perhaps less reliable, i.e., peers, mass media. Therefore, perceptions under these conditions may be less valid and of little value to the classroom instructor. This study examines the relationship between student perception of knowledge, and actual knowledge in the area of drugs.

Level of interest is also examined as a motivational factor in classroom studies. Previous studies have investigated interest and its effect on classroom achievement [5]. Interest has been found not to significantly increase achievement. Its effect depended on the nature of the task as well as characteristics of the student [6]. No study, thus far, has examined interest in terms of perceived student knowledge. This study attempts to do so.

Comments on the Report

METHOD

Two-hundred and fifty-three subjects enrolled in the 1974–1975 academic year in drug education courses in the Department of Health Education at Lehman College were sampled. The absence of specific pre-requisite courses as well as its requirement for all prospective New York State teachers resulted in a student body from various college majors. At the first class meeting, each student completed a drug knowledge and interest inventory. Categories specifying self-perceived knowledge and interest were low, moderate, or high. At the next class meeting, students were given an examination in order to assess their actual drug knowledge. For purposes of investigation, items on all three instruments were grouped into the following topical categories: Pharmacology, Terminology, Legal Aspects, Social Issues, Psychological Aspects, Prevention, Treatment, Rehabilitation, and Drugs of Abuse. The knowledge test was initially developed by the researcher in 1972. Content validity was insured by generating items from college textbooks, the New York State Drug Education Curriculum, and in consultation with experts in the field. The test originally contained 135 items. After each administration, the examination was subjected to an item analysis to determine the functioning and non-functioning foils as well as the descrimination index for each item. The test now consists of 100 items. The reliability coefficient of the latest revision is .75 and was determined by the Kuder-Richardson (KR_{21}) formula.

The knowledge and interest inventory was a revised version of *The Checklist for Knowledge and Interest in Drugs and Drug Use* [7]. Content validity was insured by employing the same criteria used for the knowledge examination. Reliability coefficients were also generated for both the knowledge and interest inventory using the KR_{21} technique. Reliability for the knowledge inventory is .79 while the reliability for the interest inventory is .85.

EXPERIMENTAL PROCEDURES

In order to generate a self-perceived drug knowledge score and an interest score for each student, a weighted value of zero, one, and two were assigned to the low, moderate, and high categories, respectively. Scores on the 100 item knowledge test ranged from 0-100. All scores were treated as continuous data. After test scores for each individual were generated, test statistics for each instrument were determined. These included mean, median, standard deviation, standard error of the mean, and reliability coefficients.

Since the main purpose of the study was to determine relationships among perception of knowledge, interest, and actual student knowledge, Pearson's Product Moment Correlation Coefficient and Analysis of variance were used. Both correlation coefficients and F-values were examined at the .05 level of significance. A sample size of 253 requires a minimum value of 1.1731 for significance of the correlation coefficient at the .05 level. Reliability scores were generated using the Kuder Richardson 21 formula. Reliability coefficients of .85 are necessary to make individual predictions but for group comparisons coefficients from .60 to .70 are acceptable.

ANALYSIS OF THE DATA

Table 1 identifies the mean, median, standard deviation, standard error and reliability for the knowledge and interest inventory and the knowledge test. As can be seen, these tests meet the reliability criterion for group predictions as stated by Levitt. The mean on the knowledge inventory was 1.32 indicating that on the average, students saw themselves as having a moderate to high level of knowledge about mood modifying substances. Further analysis by topic area indicated that there was a wide variability in perception of knowledge within the topic areas previously identified. Students perceived themselves as more knowledgeable in the areas of Social Issues, Psychological Aspects, Terminology and least knowledgeable about Legal Aspects, and Pharmacology. Student perception of their knowledge was inconsistent with the findings on the knowledge test. The mean score of 55.23 indicates a low level of student knowledge. Students perceived themselves as being more knowledgeable than they really were.

Comments on the Report

Table 1. Statistics for the Drug Knowledge and Interest Inventory and the Knowledge Test

	Perception of Knowledge	Interest	Actual Knowledge
Mean	1.32	1.13	55.23
Median	1.01	.97	61.43
Standard Deviation	.19	.32	9.84
Standard Error	.02	.02	.62
Reliability Coefficient	.81	.86	.73

Students demonstrated a high level of interest, indicative of the popularity of the subject matter. Since drugs are a prominent social issue, continually in the public's awareness, and possibly a popular past-time among some college students, many may feel that they are well-informed which is reflected in their knowledge inventory scores. In reality, the students may have much misinformation causing low scores on the knowledge test.

Table 2 may be consulted for significant correlation coefficients. As the table indicates, there was a significant relationship between interests and perception of knowledge. This was expected since a person who has strong interests in an area will seek information about his area of interest. This information, however, may be from unreliable sources and thus the student may see himself, inaccurately, as being well-informed. Surprisingly, no significant relationship was found between actual knowledge and perception of knowledge. Students do not seem to be able to accurately assess their level of knowledge. This may be due, in part, to their desire to appear more sophisticated about a popular social issue. Plus and minus one standard deviation were used to separate knowledge test scores into three distinct groups; high, moderate, and low. Correlation coefficients were then compiled for these groups. It was found that a positive and significant correlation existed between actual knowledge and perceived knowledge for those students who scored above one standard deviation. This is consistent with the literature [9].

Comments on the Report

Table 2. Correlation Coefficients for Perceived Knowledge, Actual Knowledge, and Interest

	Perception of Knowledge	Interest	Actual Knowledge
Actual Knowledge	ns	ns	1.00
Interests	.193[a]	1.00	.124

[a]Significant at the .05 level.

To further analyze relationships, analysis of variance was performed. In order to determine where differences among the groups existed, Kramer's Extension of Duncan's New Multiple Range Test for Unequal N's was performed. As was done on the knowledge test, one standard deviation above and below the mean served to divide scores into three distinct groups; high, moderate, and low on the self-perceived knowledge and interest inventory. Those students who perceived themselves as well-informed had moderate scores on the drug knowledge test. Those with moderate and low perception of knowledge scores had the lowest scores on the knowledge test.

In general, those students with high, moderate, and low interest scores tended to have high, moderate, and low scores, respectively, on the knowledge inventory. There was one exception, however, relating to marijuana. Virtually all students expressed great interest in marijuana, yet unlike the other areas, these students had moderate and low knowledge scores. This may be indicative of the misinformation of this popular topic gathered from unreliable sources.

CONCLUSIONS

Knowledge and interest inventories serve a valuable role in helping college instructors to sharpen objectives and focus student learning experiences. Though student interests may be accurately expressed, instructors must be wary of the level of knowledge as viewed by the students. Students may wish to identify themselves as knowledgeable particularly in areas in which students identify closely. Pre-testing, as exemplified by the knowledge test, serves an invaluable function in the teaching-learning experience. Those areas in which students are indeed knowledgeable may be identified and either excluded from the syllabus or examined more casually. Areas in which students are less-well-informed will also be identified and can be emphasized by the instructor.

REFERENCES

1. E. J. Doleys and G. A. Renzaglia, Accuracy of Student Prediction of College Grades, *The Personnel and Guidance Journal*, pp. 528-530, February 1963.
2. R. W. Skoger and L. A. Braskamp, Changes in Self-Rating and Life Goals as Related to Student Accomplishment in College, *ACT Research Reports*, No. 16, American College Testing Program, 1966.
3. F. C. Young, College Freshman Judge Their Own Scholastic Promise, *The Personnel and Guidance Journal*, pp. 399-403, March 1954.
4. D. A. Biggs and D. J. Tinsley, Student Made Academic Predictions, *The Journal of Educational Research*, pp. 195-197, January 1970.
5. R. B. Cattell, *Prediction and Understanding of the Effect of Children's Interest Upon School Performance*, University of Illinois, Urbana Illinois, 1961.
6. M. M. Clifford, How Learning and Liking are Related—A Clue, *Journal of Educational Psychology*, pp. 183-186, February 1973.

7. O. S. Ray, Checklist for Knowledge and Intrest in Drugs and Drug Abuse, C. V. Mosby & Company, 1972.
8. E. Levitt, *Clinical Research in the Behavioral Sciences*, Charles P. Thomas, Glencoe, Illinois, p. 57, 1961.
9. K. K. Keefer, Characteristics of Students Who Make Accurate and Inaccurate Self-Predictions of College Achievement, *The Journal of Educational Research*, pp. 401–404, June 1971.

Graduates of Secondary Schools in and Around 1900: Did Most of Them Go to College?*

This Column for Your Comments on the Report*

Edward Krug

During the past several years, published statements have appeared to the effect that most graduates of secondary schools in and around 1900 went to college. Estimated fractions run as high as two-thirds and three-fourths. Such figures have been widely accepted and are often used in discussions about policy for high schools today. A few writers have taken the opposite position and identify the college entrants of that period as a minority of the secondary-school graduates.

Most of these statements, whether on one side or the other, are presented without evidence or without suggestions as to where such evidence may be found. There is good reason for these omissions: the evidence does not lie on the surface. The *Reports* of the commissioner of education in and around 1900 do not present direct totals on this point. Some writers on both sides, however, make use of relevant indirect evidence.

Those who arrive at high rates of college-going do so by comparing the number of students in colleges with the number in secondary schools. One recent publication, for example, presents figures showing approximately 700,000 students in secondary schools and 232,000 students in undergraduate higher education for the year 1900. That is, there were about one-third as many students in colleges as in secondary schools, public and private. General citation for these totals, without specific page and volume reference, is made to *Biennial Surveys* of the Office of Education (1: 156). These totals are followed several pages later by the statement that two-thirds of the graduates of secondary schools in 1900 went to college (1: 160, 166).

Offhand, the inference of the two-thirds rate of college-going from the one-third ratio of college to secondary-school students seems a reasonable one. It is supported by the fact that secondary schools were turning out only about 70,000 graduates a year (2). To stock the colleges with 232,000 undergraduates would have

*Reprinted from *The School Review* 70: 266–72, Autumn, 1962, by permission of the University of Chicago Press. Copyright 1962 by the University of Chicago.

*See footnote to this column, p. 139.

required nearly all the graduates of secondary schools. From this reasoning it appears that the estimate of two-thirds is not too high, but if anything too low. All this depends on the assumption that the 232,000 undergraduates had come to college by way of graduation and that the institutions they attended required such graduation for entrance.

It is necessary, therefore, to see what categories of students the total of 232,000 undergraduates represents. The exact total is reported as 231,761 undergraduates in the historical summary of the *Biennial Survey* for 1954–56 (3). This is identifiable in the commissioner's *Report* for 1899–1900 (4) as the sum of the entries in the following categories for that year:

Liberal arts (or collegiate departments)		104,098
Professional		58,070
Law	12,516	
Theological	8,009	
Medical	25,213	
Dental	7,928	
Pharmaceutical	4,042	
Veterinary	362	
Students in normal schools		69,593
Total		231,761

Presumably many of the 104,098 students in collegiate departments were secondary-school graduates. The Carnegie Foundation for the Advancement of Teaching, however, pointed out in 1909 that many colleges even at that date were admitting students who had not completed secondary schooling (5). The report referred not only to secondary-school students in the preparatory departments of those institutions, but to those admitted to regular college study as Freshmen.

The report of 58,070 professional students is more doubtful from the point of view of representing secondary-school graduates. As late as 1907, only about half the regular medical schools in the country were members of the Association of American Medical Colleges, which required schools seeking entrance to that group to set an admission standard that was the equivalent of high-school graduation (6).

Even more doubtful in relation to secondary-school graduation is the category of 69,593 students in normal schools. Most of the normal schools at that time admitted students directly from the eighth grade and were in effect competitors of secondary schools (7).

It cannot be proved or even safely assumed that the 231,761 undergraduates in higher education in 1900 had come as graduates of secondary schools, public or private. Accordingly, estimates of the college-going rate of secondary-school graduates in 1900 made on the basis of secondary-school and college enrollments are inconclusive.

How sound, then, is the assertion that most graduates of secondary schools in this period did not go to college? Those who so argue may draw possible support from the commissioner's *Reports* throughout the 1890's and for 1900, although as noted previously, these reports do not give direct totals on this point (8). The *Reports* do, however, state proportions of secondary-school student bodies listed as preparing for college, either for classical or scientific courses, and the proportions of graduates listed as having been college-preparatory students. This information, summarized in Table 1, indicates that only one-seventh of the students in 1900 were preparing for college and that only one-third of the graduates had been so prepared.

Inferences from these data depend on the accuracy of the data and on the meanings of the terms used. The accuracy of the commissioner's *Reports* was often questioned during the period under consideration, although not on this point. Beyond this, there are tantalizing questions of interpretation. What was meant by a college-preparatory student? Did most of the graduates listed as

Comments on the Report

Table 1. Secondary-school Students and Secondary-School Graduates: Listings as to College Preparation

Type of school	Secondary-school students 1900			Secondary-school graduates 1900		
	Number	Number listed as preparing for college	Per cent listed as preparing for college	Number	Number listed as having been prepared for college	Per cent listed as having been prepared for college
Public	519,251	56,202	10.82	61,737	18,693	30.28
Private.	110,797	35,315	31.87	12,216	5,673	46.43
Combined . .	630,048	91,517	14.53	73,953	24,366	32.95

Commissioner of Education, *Report for the Year1899–1900*, II, 2120-22, 2125, and 2127. Washington: Bureau of Education, 1901.

college-preparatory students go to college? Were there many or some who went to college although they had not been college-preparatory students? Presumably a college-preparatory student was a student who was considered such by the person who filed the report from the local secondary school, each supplying his own definition.

It is difficult in any case to conceive the possibility that two-thirds of these graduates went to college but that only one-third of the graduating classes were known by the persons filing the reports to have been college-preparatory students. On the basis of the statistical evidence, it appears that the case for a relatively low college-going rate is better than the case for such fractions as two-thirds and three-fourths, although neither is conclusive.

There remain at least two other possible approaches to the question. One is that of using scattered state and local reports giving direct totals. Another is to examine statements and estimates made by writers and speakers in the period under inquiry.

Available state and local reports in no way constitute a statistical sample and are of interest primarily to check the inferences that may be drawn from the commissioner's *Reports*. The principal of the Denver (North Side) High School, for example, reported in 1899 that less than one-fifth (46 out of 236) of his graduates from 1886 through 1899 had gone to college or were intending to go (9). Computations made from fairly complete data in Massachusetts for 1895 indicate that slightly more than one-third of the graduates of public high schools in that year went to college, scientific school, or normal school (10). The assistant superintendent of the Chicago public schools in 1900 reported that 28 per cent of that year's class had "expressed an intention to go to college," and he went on to say that this was the highest per cent since records had been kept in that city (11). The president of the University of Wisconsin in 1896 declared that 49 per cent of high-school graduates in that state had gone to "higher institutions of one grade or another" (12). Of the various local reports for that period, the only one running as high as the modern estimates was that of the principal of the Cleveland Central High School, who said in 1900 that 80 per cent of the graduates of his school continued their studies, half of these in college or scientific school and half in normal training (13).

The writings and speeches of secondary-school and college men in that period suggest overwhelmingly that the over-all college-going rate of secondary-school graduates was even lower than the one-third rate indicated in the commissioner's *Report*. This was not a time of yes-men in education; controversy was often bitter. Yet the writers and speakers were almost unanimous on this point (14). If indeed most graduates of secondary schools in this period did go to college, it was one of the best-kept secrets of the turn of the century.

In summary, then, the argument for a high college-going rate on the part of secondary-school graduates in the period around 1900 has little to support it. The case derived from comparisons of numbers of students in colleges and secondary schools is inconclusive. In contrast, inferences of a low college-going rate drawn from the commissioner's *Reports* are supported by local surveys and by the testimony of schoolmen who wrote and talked on the subject.

Comments on the Report

Until further evidence appears, we are left with the conclusion that most of the secondary-school graduates in and around 1900, public and private, did not go to college and that they were, in the terminology of that time, finishing students, or what we would call terminal students today.

Comments on the Report

NOTES

1. *The High School in a Changing World.* Thirty-sixth Yearbook, American Association of School Administrators, p. 156. Washington: American Association of School Administrators, 1958.

2. Commissioner of Education. *Report for the Year 1899-1900*, II, 2122, 2125. Washington: Bureau of Education, 1901.

3. *Biennial Survey of Education in the United States: 1954-56; Chapter 4, Section I, Statistics of Higher Education: 1955-56*, p. 6, Washington: Office of Education, 1958.

4. Based on memorandum, July 11, 1961, from Henry G. Badger, Office of Education, in response to inquiry from the writer regarding the sources and the components of the 231,761 total. The total for liberal arts appears in II, 1878 and 1879 of the commissioner's *Report* for 1899-1900; that for professional students on page 1965; and that for normal schools on page 2067.

5. Henry S. Pritchett. "Report of the President," *Fourth Annual Report of the President and Treasurer*, pp. 134-38 and Table A, pp. 145-46. New York: Carnegie Foundation for the Advancement of Teaching, 1909.

6. William R. Williams, "The Teaching of Medicine," *Educational Review*, XXXIV (December, 1907), 468-69. See also N.P. Colwell, "Medical Education," *Biennial Survey of Education, 1916-18* (Bulletin 1919, Number 88, 1921), I, 71-72. Washington: Bureau of Education.

7. See David Felmley, "High School Preparation of Candidates for Normal-School Training," National Education Association, *Addresses and Proceedings* (1911), pp. 445-46; Joseph M. Gwinn, "Tendencies in the Entrance Requirements of State Normal Schools," *Education*, XXVIII (December, 1907), 233-37; William C. Ruediger, "Recent Tendencies in the Normal Schools of the United States," *Educational Review*, XXXIII (March, 1907), 271-87.

8. See John Francis Latimer, *What's Happened to Our High Schools?* p. 117. Washington: Public Affairs Press, 1958. Latimer recognizes that the *Reports* do not give direct figures. (See page 136, footnote 2.)

9. James H. Van Sickle, quoted in editorial, *Educational Review*, XVIII (September, 1899), 202.

10. J. W. MacDonald, *The Massachusetts High Schools, June, 1895* (Massachusetts Board of Education, Public Document No. 2, January, 1896), pp. 311-48. The rate is based on my calculations from those given for separate schools.

11. A. F. Nightingale. "Report of Assistant Superintendent in Charge of the High Schools," *Chicago Board of Education Forty-sixth Annual Report* for year ending June 20, 1900, p. 209. Chicago: Board of Education.

12. C. K. Adams. "Higher Education in the North Central States," North Central Association of Colleges and Secondary Schools, *Proceedings* (1897), p. 5.

13. Edward L. Harris. "The Cleveland Schools," *Education*, XX (February, 1900), 332.

14. See, for example, George W. Atherton, "Proposals for the Middle States," College Association of the Middle States and Maryland, *Proceedings* (1892), pp. 10-16; L. H. Austin, "The Province of the Western High School, " National Educational Association, *Addresses and Proceedings* (1892), ppl 677-87; J. Stanley Brown, "The Autonomy of the High School," National Education Association, *Addresses and Proceedings* (1909), p. 481; Arthur L. Foley, "The Subject Matter of High-School Physics," National Educational Association, *Addresses and Proceedings* (1904), p. 865; S. A. Forbes, "The Desirability of So Federating the North Central Colleges and Universities as To Secure Essentially Uniform or at Least Equivalent Entrance Requirements," North Central Association of Colleges and Secondary Schools, *Proceedings* (1901), pp. 70-71; Victor Frazee, "The Vocational Motive in the School," *Education*, XXVIII (May, 1908), 585-86; Elmer Schultz Gerhard, "Rapid Transit Education," *Education*, XXVIII (January, 1908), 295; Christopher Gregory, "Uniform College Entrance Requirements with a Common Board of Examiners," Association of Colleges and Preparatory Schools of the Middle States and Maryland, *Proceedings* (1899), p. 50; D. E. Phillips, "The Elective System in American Education," *Pedagogical Seminary*, VIII (June, 1901), 229; Lucy M. Salmon, "Unity in College Entrance History," *Educational Review*, XII (September, 1896), 167-68; R. E. Sears, "The True Function of the Public Schools," National Educational Association, *Addresses and Proceedings* (1907), p. 986; G. A. Stuart, "The Relations between High School and Elementary Schools," *Educational Review*, XXII (November, 1901), 406.

Comments on the Report

Appendix

List of Symbols and Abbreviations Frequently Encountered in Reading Research Reports

ABBREVIATIONS

AD	Average deviation
df (ndf)	Degrees of freedom, number of degrees of freedom
F	The ratio of two estimates of σ^2. The F test or F ratio
f	Frequency
f_e	Expected frequency
f_o	Observed frequency
G	Geometric mean
H	Harmonic mean
H_o	The null hypothesis
i	Class interval
k	The number of samples
Med	Median
Mo	Mode
N,n	Number of items in a sample
P	Probability of success, level of significance
$Q_1\ Q_2\ Q_3$	First, second, and third quartiles
Q	Semi-interquartile range
r	Coefficient of correlation (Pearsonian)
s	The standard deviation of a sample
SD	The standard deviation

$SE_{\bar{x}}$	The standard error of the mean
t	Student's t, t test for populations below 30.
$\overline{X}$	Arithmetic mean
x, X	Horizontal axis, variable of one kind
y, Y	Vertical axis, variable of another kind
z	Standard score

GREEK SYMBOLS USED IN RESEARCH REPORTS

Σ	Take the sum of, add
σ	The standard deviation of the population
$\hat{\sigma}$	The estimated standard deviation of the population
μ	The mean of the population
χ^2	Chi-square, a statistic showing the degree of divergence between the observed and expected frequencies
η	The correlation ratio
ϕ	Phi coefficient
τ	Kendall's tau correlation
ρ	Spearman rank–order correlation

SYMBOLS USED IN RESEARCH REPORTS

$\sqrt{}$	The square root, take the square root of (whatever is under the bar).
$>$	is greater than
$<$	is less than
$\gg$	is very much larger than
$\ll$	is very much less than
$\geqslant$	is greater than or equal to
$\leqslant$	is less than or equal to
∞	infinity, infinitely large
$|a|$	the absolute value of a without regard to $+$ or $-$ signs
$=$	equals, equal to
$\neq$	does not equal, not equal to
$!$	factorial i.e., $3!$ means $3 \times 2 \times 1 = 6$

Index